DIGITAL DIVISIONS

DIGITAL DIVISIONS

—

*How Schools
Create Inequality in
the Tech Era*

—

MATTHEW H. RAFALOW

THE UNIVERSITY OF CHICAGO PRESS
Chicago and London

The University of Chicago Press, Chicago 60637
The University of Chicago Press, Ltd., London
© 2020 by Matthew H. Rafalow
Published 2020
Printed in the United States of America

29 28 27 26 25 24 23 22 21 20   1 2 3 4 5

ISBN-13: 978-0-226-72655-7 (cloth)
ISBN-13: 978-0-226-72669-4 (paper)
ISBN-13: 978-0-226-72672-4 (e-book)
DOI: https://doi.org/10.7208/chicago/9780226726724.001.0001

Library of Congress Cataloging-in-Publication Data

Names: Rafalow, Matthew H., author.
Title: Digital divisions : how schools create inequality in the tech era /
Matthew H. Rafalow.
Description: Chicago : University of Chicago Press, 2020. |
Includes bibliographical references and index.
Identifiers: LCCN 2020005373 | ISBN 9780226726557 (cloth) |
ISBN 9780226726694 (paperback) | ISBN 9780226726724 (ebook)
Subjects: LCSH: Educational technology—United States—Case studies. |
Digital divide—United States—Case studies. | Educational equalization—
United States—Case studies.
Classification: LCC LB1028.43.R337 2020 | DDC 371.33—dc23
LC record available at https://lccn.loc.gov/2020005373

♾ This paper meets the requirements of
ANSI/NISO Z39.48-1992 (Permanence of Paper).

CONTENTS

INTRODUCTION

One of my first visits to Heathcliff Academy was to observe Ms. Lawson's sixth-grade history class. Heathcliff, a private school located in Southern California, had a hefty ticket for entry. With no available scholarships, this limited enrollment to the wealthy and White families living in its vicinity. The flow of income allowed the school to buy and provide iPads to all its students. Not only could students use them in class, but they could take them home, too. In this particular class, students were using iPads to work on a project where they explained and critiqued an international news story.

"All right, my little historians!" exclaimed Ms. Lawson. "Let's take those iPads out. It's time to continue work on our news presentation." Students all reached into their bags and turned their tablets on. As I peeked at a nearby student's screen, I watched as she opened Keynote, a slideshow presentation app native to Apple devices. Ms. Lawson walked around the classroom to help a few students find and open Keynote to get ready for the activity. "You all know what to do," she said. "Your final presentation is due next week."

The classroom was, for the most part, relatively quiet as students swiped and tapped around their iPad screens. But just a few minutes into the working session, a loud pop beat blasted from a student's iPad and cut through the silence. I quickly realized that the sound was coming from the same nearby student I saw opening the presentation app. She rapidly swiped on the screen to close a music video by Katy Perry, a pop musician. The class chuckled, and even Ms. Lawson cracked a smile. "Juliana," she said knowingly. "I hope Ms. Perry will be making an appearance in your news presentation next week." Juliana grinned and nodded. Ms. Lawson turned to the rest of the class. "Folks, if what you're doing makes noise, please keep the volume low or pull out some earphones." Shortly thereafter, I noticed some students swiping to a web browser to look up images of recording artists, a couple even copying and pasting their photos into their Keynote presentations, too.

A few short weeks later, I made my first visit to Sheldon Junior High to observe Ms. Bartow's sixth-grade music class. She had told me beforehand that they were using software to learn how to compose music for a class project. Although only a forty-minute drive from Heathcliff, the school served a very different student population. Once an area for predominately White families, the outlying neighborhood had rapidly shifted in the past ten years to accommodate an influx of Asian American immigrant families, mostly middle class. Their children increasingly populated the school district.

Though Sheldon was a public school, its teachers and administrators went to considerable lengths to ensure that up-to-date digital technologies were readily available for instruction. This was certainly apparent when I visited to observe Ms. Bartow's classroom. Arriving first, I made my way to the edge of the room and sat in a chair with a view of the whole space. Looking around, I counted five sections with four pristine computers in each; the monitors were large and high resolution, not unlike those I see professional designers use in my own work in the tech industry.

A young man, clad in a jean vest and rainbow sneakers, walked into the room not long after I had sat down. He passed me on the way to his seat, pausing to introduce himself as Luke. "This class is great!" he said in a poorly delivered whisper. "My song is gonna be the best." He eventually took his seat in front of a computer, and just as the bell rang, Ms. Bartow and the remaining students shuffled into the room and sat down at their desks. "Okay, everyone," Ms. Bartow said. "Let's get to it!" I looked around as students put on headphones and opened their work. Their screens were filled with horizontal lines, and they dragged and dropped little music notes to form their compositions. I was astonished at how quiet the room was for a music class, aside from a constant staccato of computer mouse clicks. Students repeatedly played back their compositions as they revised them, but their headphones muffled the noise almost entirely.

Ms. Bartow waved me over to her desk, indicating that she wanted to show something on her computer. "Get a load of this," she said. I saw roughly twenty tiny boxes arranged on her screen and upon a closer look realized that they were all miniature versions of computer screens. They were moving in real time. "Isn't this wild?" she said. "I can watch what they're doing on their computers, and I don't even have to patrol around the room." Indeed, the screens looked not too different from a series of surveillance cameras. Students mostly seemed to be using the music composition software for their class project. "Look here," she said, pointing to one of the tiny windows. She clicked it. It expanded to show a hip hop music video playing in a small browser window. "Watch this," she said with a smirk. Ms. Bartow then stood up from her chair and yelled, "Hey! LUKE! Stop watching that video and get back to work!" Luke was stunned. After a moment, I could see from Ms. Bartow's expanded screen that Luke had closed the music video. He quickly got back to work on music composition.

What's particularly interesting about these examples is that both of these sixth-grade classes were focused on a creative activity for learning. At Heathcliff, students were creating a digital presentation about the news, and at Sheldon, they were working on a music project using composition software. Both classes had the latest in digital technology to complete their activities, and classroom time at each was to be used for independent work. The similarities end here. This same activity— a student opening a music video—was interpreted by both teachers differently. Although the class itself was centered on making music, Ms. Bartow publicly sanctioned students for watching music videos for fun, even if it didn't distract other students. Ms. Lawson, however, incorporated students' broad interests in digital media into their news project. These teachers weren't alone in their digital approaches. As I documented classroom life at both schools over the course of an academic year, I found that disciplining digital play in this way was the go-to pedagogical practice at Sheldon Junior High, whereas actively incorporating kids' playful pursuits online into academic work was commonplace at Heathcliff Academy. Why did teachers construct the value of similar technologies and kids' digital play so differently?

As I carried out this project, adding even another middle school for comparison, I tried to sort all of this out. Although I have always been a bit of a technophile, I have been leery of public perception of digital technologies as a "magic bullet" to address the ills of society. Social science showed me a host of structures that impose barriers to educational equity even before laptops and social media entered the equation. I believe that a researcher who visits digital-era schools will still observe, as I did, many hallmarks from classic studies of day-to-day school life. When school bells ring, a campus rapidly transforms from a silent sanctuary into a bustling hub powered by an energetic, swift-moving crowd. Teachers share idle gossip in the faculty lounge. Students cluster off during lunchtime and chat variously about homework and the latest peer dramas. But the contemporary ethnographer will notice some significant differences from school ethnographies of even a decade ago.

Digital technologies are everywhere: nearly all students and faculty carry mobile devices like smartphones, and classrooms are equipped with computers and even interactive whiteboards. In the words of one teacher, internet access is "like oxygen."

As schools are catching up to the digital age, we are witness to a nationwide effort to close gaps in access to technology, also known as the "digital divide," in a move to give young people from all strata of society the opportunity to develop and share their talents. Schools are exponentially ramping up for the digital era with both curricular reforms and investments in high-quality hardware and software. Through the assistance of local, state, and federal grants, as well as corporate philanthropy, school districts spend $17 billion annually on instructional technology.[1]

The exact technologies purchased vary widely by district, but they often include high-speed internet access. Hardware purchases typically include computer labs, mobile devices like laptops and tablets, and interactive whiteboards. Software investments are composed of online learning management systems, electronic student portfolio databases, grading tools, educational games, and licenses to file-sharing services. Longitudinal studies on the state of the digital divide in education show that these investments are working.[2] The biggest disparities in access to necessary hardware and software, both at the school level and among families, have shrunk dramatically in recent years. For education reformers, the holy grail of one laptop per child is a more likely reality than ever before.

Educators know that the goal is not just to bring schools' resources up to parity. As a consequence of vastly unequal childhoods, students show up at school with different advantages. This presents challenges to teaching.[3] Fortunately, there's good news on this front: young people may already have a leg up because they use many digital technologies with friends. Demographic analyses consistently show an impressive level of parity in digital technology adoption among young people.[4] For decades, the story from educational research has been that children have unequal access to important resources needed for school success, particularly along lines of student race-ethnicity and social class.[5] In the contemporary moment, however, we find minimal differences between young people with respect to their access to internet and internet-connected devices like computers and smartphones. These rates of technology adoption among youth have far surpassed those of older generations of adults.

Some educational movements have been revitalized by young adults' rapid adoption of digital technologies. Their proponents argue that the digital skills children develop through play with peers online are essential to learning and achievement in the twenty-first century. Research in this vein finds that children use digital technologies as an extension of their youth culture; hanging out with peers requires basic proficiencies in online communication and using digital tools to create and share media online.[6] To scholars of so-called digital literacies, these skills could be nurtured in and outside of schools and foster educational achievement and later mobility in the new economy. Teachers may benefit from familiarity with the digital technology skills that young people bring to school and thus be better able to support working-class students and students of color who also have these skills.

A recent school technology rollout, however, suggests that the issue may be not simply whether kids have key technology skills, but rather what skills are counted as valuable for educational achievement. When in 2013 Los Angeles Unified School District (LAUSD) signed a $30 million deal with Apple to buy iPads for its 650,000 students, the district believed it was reducing a major obstacle to learning. Superintendent John Deasy heralded the move as a civil rights initiative designed to give students—mostly students of color from low-income families—access to a tool needed for success in the twenty-first century.[7]

Within a week of the rollout, students found ways to bypass security software so that they could access social media like Facebook and Twitter and watch videos on YouTube. These hacks made national news. Rather than explicitly using the school-provided iPads for standardized tests and to do homework, students also wanted to use them for fun. As a result, the iPad initiative was deemed a complete failure: an "iFail." The iPads were revoked, a lead technology integrationist at the district resigned, and LAUSD demanded their money back for Apple's inability to protect the purchased hardware from their own students. For the district, fun was a major threat to proper learning.

What's interesting about the LAUSD iPad debacle is that gaps in students' skills were not the issue. Students were skilled enough at digital tinkering to bypass software created by sophisticated programmers. Reports suggest, too, that these students were pro-social enough to teach each other how to modify the software so they could play with their friends online. In fact, these activities do not seem much different from fabled stories of digital tinkering by innovators like Apple's Steve Jobs, Facebook's Mark Zuckerberg, or Google's Sergey Brin and Larry Page: young people peeked under the hood of the hardware and worked diligently to modify the platform for their own purposes. Students found creative ways to repurpose the iPad and make it more relevant to them. Why are these students described as "hackers" and not innovators?

The question of who gets to be an innovator seems worthy of exploration. Under pressure from activists, Silicon Valley released reports that show the profoundly unequal distribution of employees in major technology companies. In 2014, Apple, Google, Facebook, and Twitter were 70 percent male. Less studied are racial-ethnic divides: at Google, for example, only 3 percent of workers are Hispanic and 2 percent are Black.[8] Although these statistics do not show the socioeconomic origins of Silicon Valley's workforce, they suggest a problem of representation along lines of gender, race, and likely social class. Critics argue that the primarily White and male Silicon "bubble" is a major problem, not only for equality, but for capitalism in general.[9]

If White and male designers' creative visions are limited to their milieu, then the remaining 69 percent of the United States population is marketed digital innovations that aren't particularly innovative for their life circumstances. Both activists and capitalists would agree, then, that diversity in the tech sector is important.

Confusion still arises around the question of why so few people of color make it into this high-tech innovation space. Hiring managers in the tech sector cite the same digital skills gap that academics worry about, claiming that there are few talented prospects to fill out their ranks. But as I try to imagine students' pathways to roles as tinkerers, I keep thinking back to the "iFail" at LAUSD. These Black and Latinx youth, largely from the working class, clearly show signs of nascent digital skills, perhaps as a consequence of their out-of-school, peer-driven activities with friends online. What do teachers and administrators, many of whom are likely to be less digitally adept than their pupils, think of their students' digital youth culture? Do they see young people's creative tendencies online as valuable for school, or not? If they do, how exactly are teachers able to cultivate students' innovative potential in practice? And where do teachers' notions of students-as-innovators come from?

To assess whether and how schools are preparing students for the digital age, we need to take a careful look at day-to-day life in today's technologically equipped classrooms. We need to assess how teachers at these schools conceive of the value of digital technology for achievement and use technological tools during instruction. Digital divides, while worrisome, are only one roadblock to students' potential, and documenting teachers' perceptions and practices will enhance our understanding of innovators' geneses beyond more simplistic garage theories.

In order to address potential obstacles faced by people of color and the less financially well off, we also require good comparison cases: we need to see if schools with high-quality technologies that vary demographically invoke similar or different perceptions of students' digital culture and capacity as innovators. Moreover, we need to assess where these classed and racialized perceptions come from without falling into familiar tropes that blame individual teachers for discriminatory beliefs.

In this book, I wrestle with these questions and ultimately make two claims that build on existing scholarship on education, technology, and innovation. Most contemporary theorizing about digital divides focuses on the importance of fostering in students key digital skills, or digital literacies, for success, like online collaboration and computer programming. If teachers are better able to transmit these skills, scholars argue, then students have a better shot at maximizing their potential in a technologically sophisticated labor market. Further, the increasing availability of digital technologies, both at school and in the homes of young people, levels the playing field with respect to access to certain resources regardless of student social origin. This allows us to test theories of unequal childhoods and theories of cultural inequality in education in that schools could potentially lift up working-class students and students of color by capitalizing on the digital know-how these less privileged students bring with them to school. Alternatively, teachers might not see these digital skills developed from play as valuable to learning, instead surveilling student usage and dismissing its potential.

I ultimately argue that the way educational institutions cultivate innovators is through their capacity to discipline play. Digital youth culture is rich with new ideas, forms, and styles. But schools set the terms for whether students can mobilize their playful digital pursuits for achievement, and they do so differently by student class and race. At schools serving primarily working- and middle-class youth of color, teachers communicate to students that their digital play is not valuable for learning. At a school serving wealthy and White youth, teachers communicate to students that their digital play is integral to learning and achievement. Thus, teachers treat kids' similar forms of digital play quite differently, with consequences for school achievement.

Disciplinary orientations to digital youth culture and play come from a complex mixture of perceptions and expectations within the school setting. This is the second claim I put forth. Teachers make assumptions about kids' potential for learning based on their race and class, and the culture of the workplace is even more important in shaping teachers' approaches to their students' digital play—just ask any teacher to share some of the "war stories" about their work in different teaching environments.

Schools host a shared set of expectations that inform how teachers perceive one another and even their own pupils. For example, I find that whether teachers' workplaces are variably hostile or family-like informs teachers' disciplinary orientations. Teachers trying to get by in a hostile work environment see their peers and their students as threats. They then link these expectations with racialized images of Asian students as hackers rather than model minorities. Teachers at a school that fosters family-like support among faculty and in teaching see their Latinx students as benevolent and hardworking immigrants rather than as future gang members. The dynamics of school workplaces render "sensible" particular racialized and classed imagery that teachers use to frame their students. They drive the very orientations to play that enable or constrain opportunities for student innovation. In other words, whether or not teachers individually stereotype their students, the culture of their workplace makes stereotypes into policy.

Education reformers, practitioners, and families who want the best for their young people are keen to prioritize the closing of digital divides at school in order to maximize students' potential. Adults probably assume that, as "digital youth,"[10] students will pay more attention in class and learn key digital skills if high-quality education technologies are more available. But we know less about how innovation works than we think. It's not just about the skills. Schools organize the sandboxes within which ideas get circulated, elevated, or shot down.

INNOVATION AND PLAY

Play is a subject of theoretical interest for philosophers, educators, and contemporary technologists. Plato argued that play is the best means by which children voluntarily learn "law-abiding" mores.[11] Johan Huizinga, writing on ancient cultures, saw play as among the purest aesthetic events, a means to express the capacity of the mind and leave one's mark upon the world.[12] This "mark" on society, as play theorists suggest, is essentially innovation. It's no surprise, then, that play periodically emerges in history as a valued social practice for learning and introducing novelty in business.

Michael Schrage, a lead technologist at the MIT Media Lab, advocates taking play into the everyday work settings that digital tinkerers inhabit.[13] He uses the example of prototyping to show the benefits of play in corporate environments. Prototypes are sketches or semifunctional applications of a new idea. Schrage finds that the selection process for who gets to play with the ideas that lead to prototyping varies across companies. When companies take play *seriously*, he argues, they construct prototyping scenarios that consider the value-added of the players and the learning affordances of frequent (and early) failures. Innovation happens when players voluntarily and eagerly participate in drawing up and revising mockups of new possibilities.

Scholars of youth culture take play seriously, too. In the largest mixed-methods study of its kind, Mizuko Ito and her colleagues document how digital technologies, when located in the hands of young people and the playful pursuits of their youth cultures, can become artifacts for new innovations.[14] Through digitally mediated play, young people "hang out" with their peers online and "mess around" with digital tools necessary for using these online sites for engagement. For example, youth use image, audio, and video editing software to remix and share their favorite media from popular culture, or tinker with design and programming embedded in online applications to find new ways to play video games. Those youth who maintain strong interests in a given activity are more prone to "geeking out," or prototyping and developing new cultural forms online that others can benefit from and celebrate.

What I take from play theorists is that play, as a social practice, represents engagement with social structure. It is a process through which people can go under the hood of the car and see, if even for a moment, what makes society work. Take, for example, a young person playing *SimCity 2000*, a city-building simulation game. In a study of the game's use for learning, Ito describes one scene where a youth playing the game tries to save money for his city by cutting all tax revenue from public services, like fire departments.[15] Although the youth enjoyed short-term gains in city income, he found himself at a loss when a fire in a corner of his city was uncontainable, and as a result he suffered more financial losses in the long term. Gameplay presented opportunities to see relationships between social structures, like financial policies and government entities, and outcomes like urban disasters. Players, too, can hit the reset button and start over to imagine a new reality with different structures in place that govern city life. Rarely in our day-to-day lives do we have the luxury of a reset button. Games can provide players with sociological foresight.

Scholars also know that play can be constructed in different ways and for different purposes. Play can be used to exert social control. Marx, like play theorists, believed that humans possess creative impulses that have great potential for connection and understanding.[16] He argued that those impulses are often controlled by powerful people who inhibit both equality and innovation. In his time, Marx saw workers coerced into using technology only as a means for material production toward capitalist ends. By selling their labor to a factory—clocking in and out, day after day—workers alienated their creative power from their own needs in order to earn a wage.

We can imagine use of digital technologies following a similar logic. Rather than working on innovations to ameliorate the ails of society, programmers could become a new generation of mindless worker bees supplementing the ends of major tech companies. Instead of providing opportunities for everyone to play, tech companies could ensure that only a privileged few could become twenty-first-century makers and tinkerers. Working-class youth and students of color may have great creative potential, but they would participate in the innovation process only as rule followers rather than game changers. As I will argue, Marxist perspectives hold a lot of truth for the reality of schooling. Play's value varies depending on school context, with different effects by the race and class of the student population.

PLAY AT SCHOOL

While Marx suggests that creativity and play can be usurped by institutions, sociologist Pierre Bourdieu provides some direction as to how schools might do this in practice.[17] A Bourdieuian perspective would treat students' digital play, and the skills they develop from play, as potential cultural capital for achievement. In this view, kids' digital know-how could potentially be legitimized by teachers during day-to-day instruction. These digital skills may be a cultural resource for participation in other aspects of kids' lives, such as their youth culture, but would be useful for school only if institutional agents, like teachers, deem them important.

As the cultural reproduction argument goes, more privileged families teach their children forms of knowledge that are valued by educational institutions, and less privileged families do not because they are not as connected to the dominant milieu. Teachers then selectively validate students who display familiarity with institutionalized signals for inclusion and exclusion, such as tastes for high culture or behaviors in line with shared expectations. Studies find over and over that children arrive at schools with different sets of habits and dispositions that are met unequally by teachers and systematically provide advantages to middle- and upper-class White children.[18]

To reduce these inequalities and increase cultural mobility, researchers argue that schools should provide disadvantaged children access to these idealized cultural resources.[19] Following the logic of Bourdieu's theory, education researchers lament that by early childhood, privileged children have already developed many key literacies that kids living in disadvantage do not receive. If we could level the playing field by providing children from every family background with cultural competencies needed for success, then disadvantaged youth could better compete with their peers.

From a cultural mobility perspective, digital youth culture presents a terrific opportunity. Research shows that major generational differences in technology adoption and digital participation have developed over the past decade.[20] Although this will change as cohorts of youth age, young people are, at present, faster adopters of digital technology than older adults. Parents are not yet the source of students' digital skills. Bourdieu does not fully elaborate on what teachers might do if kids from various class backgrounds all share potentially valuable competencies for schooling. How might teachers evaluate the digital skills that youth bring to school?

I will argue that disciplining play is one means by which institutions act as gatekeepers, leading to unequal student outcomes. Teachers at privileged schools enable their students' digital play to be used for achievement in class, sometimes even deferring to kids' fun ideas in place of existing class lessons. Meanwhile, teachers at schools serving less privileged youth favor institutionally imposed rules that subordinate students' creativity. Sociologists of education provide us with some clues as to how teachers do this in practice. Institutions control innovation through their capacity to discipline play.

DISCIPLINING PLAY

Social reproduction theorists argue that institutions exert powerful control over the creative potential of young people. These scholars get more granular about how schools might factor into this process. To do this, they offer a definition of "discipline" that is somewhat different from popular notions of finger-waving and ruler-rapping. As a consequence of class- and race-based attitudes toward students, schools differently imagine their students' potential. These shared beliefs among teachers are enacted through discipline. The term refers not simply to the correction of students' bad behavior but also to an institutional process that determines appropriate behavior and instills norms into students. In this view, schools transmit messages to students in ways that inform classroom practice and even students' perceptions of their own academic worth.

Samuel Bowles and Herbert Gintis provide the most thorough explanation of how discipline works in school settings.[21] Although primarily focused on social class (and not race), they argue that schools differently imagine labor market trajectories of their students. Teachers give praise and rewards, like better grades, to students who conform to school-specific ideals. They punish nonconformers with lower grades and other signs of disapproval, like public shame. Here, discipline refers to *both* the rewards and the sanctions. Discipline is the means by which schools instill a "built-in supervisor" in students. Schools aid in the production of particular types of student consciousness.

Considerable work documents the various orientations to students that teachers exhibit based on shared beliefs about students' class and race.[22] For example, schools that serve working-class youth provide guidance for obtaining only working-class jobs. By contrast, schools serving privileged youth provide them with information about elite schools.[23] In another example, Mexican American youth are told their Mexican-influenced culture, including Spanish language use, Spanish-sounding names, and approaches to learning favored by Mexican schools, are useless for achievement in the United States.[24] I later argue that research on teacher perceptions is complicated by the fact that beliefs are shaped by organizational constraints. Ultimately, social reproduction theorists' original argument still holds: teachers imagine the potential of their students according to where they "fit" in a stratified labor market, and subsequently enact those perceptions through instruction.

What's fascinating is how instructors do this in the digital era. Teachers told me that they, like many in our society, do not know what the economic future of our country will be during the digital age—they can only speculate. Their speculations, however, were linked to older models of the labor market and included who gets to be innovators and game-changers in that economy. Teachers then enacted those perceptions, with good intents, during their pedagogical practices with digital technologies. Through discipline, schools constructed students as particular types of technology users.

I build on social reproduction theories by illustrating how schools manage students' creativity by disciplining play. This study benefited from a fascinating time when students, regardless of family origin, shared a similar baseline of digital skills because of digital youth cultural participation. Young people's digital play, for example on social media and through video games, can be transformed by teachers into valuable cultural capital for achievement. More than that, teachers can learn from students. Discipline is the process by which teachers determine which students' digital play matters for school. Students of color and working-class youth were told their digital play was either irrelevant or threatening to schooling, whereas privileged youth were encouraged, if not required, to play at school for success. Consequently, students internalized different boundaries between play and educational institutions: youth differently reported digital play at school as useless, anxiety inducing, or paramount for their development in school.

TEACHERS' PERCEPTIONS

In the first part of this book, I argue that schools differently discipline play in ways that shape students' ability to innovate within institutions. The second claim I make gets at where these disciplinary orientations come from. Although social reproduction theorists correctly observe the stratified effects of schooling, they do not well substantiate the origins of teachers' imagined labor outcomes for their students. This matters because these perceptions are said to shape pedagogical practice.

But mapping out where teachers' perceptions of their students came from turned out to be quite the puzzle. As I asked the primarily White middle-class teachers in this study to reflect on student populations they have taught, at both their present place of work and other schools, I found that they all shared two competing views of their students of color, two ways of perceiving working-class Latinx students, and two constructions of middle-class Asian American students. At a school serving mostly working-class Latinx kids, teachers described their students as "benevolent immigrants," while saying that Latinx students they worked with elsewhere were "future gang members." Faculty at a school serving mostly middle-class Asian American students said their students were "cutthroat hackers," whereas Asian students they taught elsewhere were "model minorities." Teachers had no such stereotypes for their White students.

Such beliefs—varied assumptions about students of color and the invisibility of Whiteness—are consistent with theories of colorblind racism. This contemporary racial ideology gives Whites a set of tools to "not see color" but at the same time exhibit really troubling racist beliefs and practices (such as racial stereotyping) that benefit Whites at the expense of people of color.[25] But theories of colorblind racism did not help me disentangle the way these faculty made sense of the multiple stereotypes they possessed about similar student demographics. Both sets of culturally racist imagery certainly exist in our society, but theories of race and racism do not explain how teachers' perceptions could be so contradictory and yet still produce unequal outcomes.

The teachers in this study helped guide me to the missing piece in this puzzle. As I followed what grounded teachers' perceptions of their students, I also heard, in tandem, many stories about teachers' workplaces. Faculty described some schools they had worked at as stressful "hell holes" where teachers ganged up against one another, and others as more pleasant, supportive environments. Incidentally, a growing body of work suggests that educators' shared culture may have a role in shaping how teachers construct their students by race and class. Though largely quantitative, this research shows that, for example, schools with collaborative teacher dynamics have fewer race and class gaps in achievement than schools with less collaborative faculty norms.[26]

As teachers walked me through the ins and outs of their workplaces, I found that each school had shared expectations of faculty that shaped their perceptions not only of each other but also of their students. Teachers at a school serving mostly working-class Latinx students described the faculty and administrators there as "in it together"; faculty at a school serving mostly middle-class Asian American students described their peers as instead "every man for himself"; and teachers at the mostly wealthy and White private school pointed to a shared expectation of elite servitude. These workplace dynamics, which were experienced by faculty as just part of the job, are what scholars of organizations refer to broadly as organizational culture.[27] But researchers have not examined the ways such workplace dynamics might actually inform teachers' perceptions of their students.[28]

In this book, I provide needed qualitative analysis to explicate how and why workplace norms among faculty structure disciplinary orientations to their students' digital play. I document how the different workplace dynamics at each school provide an orienting framework for the "appropriate" belief as it aligns with teachers' workplace norms. At a school with hostile faculty relations, teachers similarly construct their students as hostile and draw on imagery of "Tiger Mom"-raised, cutthroat hackers to describe their Asian American students. At a school with family-like faculty relations, teachers likewise invoke missionary-like paternalism and view their Latinx students as benevolent, hardworking immigrants trying to get ahead. But consistent with theories of race and racism, White students evade the effects of racialized perceptions because Whiteness is invisible. The successes and failures of White students were seen as individual and not as a consequence of their racial affiliation as they were for students of color.

THE STUDY

At present, digital technology may be largely foreign to sociological research, but schools are certainly within its purview. Sociologists of education employ the gamut of research methods to document and understand social life in schools, and ethnographic methods are valuable for capturing how structures operate in day-to-day life. When I embarked on this study, I was interested in exploring the relationship between youth culture and schooling in the twenty-first century. By looking at the school ecology, rather than just teachers *or* children, I hoped to capture interactions between people broadly connected to schooling and explore how they shaped the perceived value and uses of digital technology for achievement. My comparative approach also meant moving beyond a small set of classrooms to understand how schools may differently integrate digital technologies for learning.

This book is based on in-depth "naturalistic" observations in three middle schools (two public, one private) that all have comparable, high-quality digital technologies available but vary by student class and race (see the appendix for more details on method). Heathcliff Academy is a private school serving mostly wealthy and White students. Sheldon Junior High is a public school with mostly middle-class Asian American students. And César Chávez Middle School has mostly working-class Latinx students. All three schools are located in suburbs near a large western city.

Middle school is an understudied and yet important experience for students for both psychological and sociological reasons. First, it is portrayed as a critical period for students' identity development and a predictor for later academic trajectories in schools.[29] Second, tracking is less likely to structure student experience, as it typically occurs later in high school.[30] Third and finally, middle school is increasingly targeted as a time for teaching key digital skills like online collaboration and production.[31] I gained access to these three schools through direct outreach with the principals about participation as part of a larger study of schools and the deployment of digital technology for learning.

It is a lot of work to effectively document school life in three schools at the same time. At the beginning of the 2013–14 school year I began by interviewing as many teachers, administrators, and staff as possible at each of the schools, thereafter observing interviewed teachers' classrooms on rotation until the end of the academic year. I typically spent a full day at one school (approximately six hours), and then a full day at another school. I randomized teachers' names to ensure that my observations were distributed equally at each school. In total, I observed just over six hundred hours in the field split evenly between the schools. I ultimately draw from 67 interviews with teachers (reflecting approximately 80 percent of each school's teacher population), each typically lasting an hour. Most teachers were interviewed a second time by the end of the year to discuss questions that came up during observation. Teachers exhibit a similar spectrum of important characteristics at each school, including years taught, technology training, and education (more details in the appendix).

As part of my fieldwork, I also attended faculty meetings and workshops and parent-teacher and after-school events, and I also observed faculty lounges and student lunch areas. During the last few months of the study, I selected one "ideal type" eighth-grade classroom at each school where the observed school-level patterns were strongest, and I randomly selected half of the students to interview. This yielded a sample of forty students. These interviews took place at the school in a room or part of the classroom where the teacher or other students could not hear our conversations. Although these interviews represent a proportionately smaller subset of the student body than I had been able to secure with faculty and staff, this sampling method allowed me to speak with youth in classes that were best fits for the school-level themes that I identified.

Teachers often expressed initial worry that they themselves would not provide the best examples of classroom technology use. In fact, teachers at each school spanned a similar range of technology skill levels, from novice to expert. When I introduced myself to teachers, I said that while I myself am "geeky," I believed that researchers have not adequately tried to understand teachers' own perspectives on both the opportunities and the challenges of technology use in daily life at school. This often broke the ice rather quickly: I learned that teachers have many, many opinions about digital technology's usefulness, and I would often hear stories about technology "fails" and their wish-lists for new products (". . . and you can go and tell *that* to Google!").

Teachers required considerably more work for me to slip into the background than did students. The potentially most obtrusive moments were during classroom observation, where I would sit in the back of the classroom behind the class. I worried that students might be concerned that someone was watching them but soon learned that classroom observations were a routine practice at each of the schools. At Heathcliff and Chávez, students would often come up to me, ask what I was studying, and weigh in on the topic of technology. As I will discuss in greater depth, Sheldon posed more challenges for establishing rapport with students. Teachers at Sheldon would periodically ask me to participate, as many adults there do, by walking around the room and monitoring students' work on computers. Wherever possible, I avoided this "surveillance" work. During appropriate moments, I tried to position myself more as a peer by talking with students to identify shared interests, like video games.

OUTLINE OF THE BOOK

My treatment of social reproduction in educational institutions is one that explores how schools can produce different realities for their students, irrespective of young people's digital skills and capacity as creative thinkers and innovators. I look for similarities and differences in why teachers sought to use new technologies for learning and in how they cultivated their students for the future. I focus on the challenges teachers face, variously from their students, parents, district officials, and from other teachers, and I examine how students make sense of the messages they receive about their own potential as budding technologists. By following these circuits of messaging between teachers and students, I illustrate how social forces inform a very early part of the pipeline in the development of future makers and tinkerers. While digital tools are important artifacts in each school, this project is a study of kids' *play* and how teachers see its value—social systems animate teachers' interpretations of play, whether or not digital tools are involved, rendering it a sociological phenomenon worthy of study.

In chapter 1, I provide a descriptive portrait and brief history of the three middle schools in the study. While serving very different student populations, each is similarly equipped with the latest in digital technologies, but they use those technologies quite differently. Chapter 2 explores how young people develop digital skills through playful pursuits online with their peers and how schools differently value those skills. Teachers discipline play, but in contrasting ways and with varying levels of effectiveness. Working-class and minoritized students' digital play is deemed either irrelevant or threatening to school, whereas privileged White students' digital forms are transformed into cultural capital for achievement. Teachers also incorporate "hip" digital youth culture into their lessons . . . but only from privileged students, allowing the institution to appear cutting edge.

In chapter 3, I examine the origins of teachers' disciplinary orientations, making connections between beliefs teachers bring to school and the norms imposed upon them by their surroundings. These linkages effectively augment schooling, driving the aforementioned disciplinary approaches to student innovation. Chapter 4 turns from questions about the sources of teaching practices to their effects on students' consciousness. I bring to the surface patterns in how students narrate their experiences over the course of middle school, including how they process teacher messaging documented in earlier chapters. I flesh out how youth either resist or conform to teacher expectations, and in doing so excavate how schooling shapes their association between schoolwork and play online. Ultimately, I show how schools shape kids' online behavior within and outside of school, with potential implications for their success later in life.

In the conclusion, I revisit the general question of the influence that institutions have on the imagined value and subsequent uses of digital technologies. I point to important ways that culture does not appear to structure these uses. Overall, however, I identify important ways that cultural phenomena animate digital technologies for teaching and differently construct students as future innovators. I conclude with possible interventions based on these findings, both for pedagogical practice and in the design of learning technologies, that may increase the chances for young people to more equally see and enact their creative worth online and offline. This book makes visible the potential of play through a study of how it surfaces when teachers and students interact at school.

1

SIMILAR TECHNOLOGIES,

DIFFERENT SCHOOLS

School ethnographers often have vivid memories of their first few field visits. Although scholarship on education technology is a relatively new literature, I was armed for my first visits with a set of rough hypotheses from a century of work on the sociology of education. Scholars have long argued that race and class are strong predictors of academic success. The proposed causes vary but include differences in neighborhoods, school resources, and pedagogical approaches. Although the schools in this study all had access to high-quality education technologies and a stated mission to integrate them into teaching, sociological priming led me to expect that I would see digital technologies used largely as paperweights in schools serving less-affluent students of color.

I was wrong. As I toured the halls of César Chávez Middle School, a school serving predominantly working-class Latinx youth, I saw digital technologies literally everywhere. They were actively being used by students and teachers alike. Nearly every room was equipped with an interactive whiteboard. iPad carts were often out and being used by students at their desks. Teachers showed me an online system they used between classes and after school to regularly communicate with students about assignments and help answer questions that came up. "A lot of schools like this don't have the resources we have," explained Ms. Bryant, the school technology manager. "We consider ourselves very fortunate and really believe that technology can help these kids prepare for the future."

What was particularly stunning was that Heathcliff Academy, a private school primarily serving White wealthy youth just about thirty

miles away, was similar in both technology saturation and digital out-
look. "I mean, it's the way of the future," explained Mr. Crouse, the
school technology manager. "To not integrate technology at school is
to not *teach* them in the twenty-first century. It's how we ensure their
later success." Like Chávez, Heathcliff had iPads widely available for
its students. Both schools also shared pedagogical commitments to
teaching digital skills like information searching, website creation,
and programming, and both purchased the latest in educational software for classroom management and teaching. If a learning scientist
were to survey teachers and students at both schools, they would be
delighted to find that despite student racial-ethnic and socioeconomic
differences, school-level gaps in technology availability and digitally
minded instruction were seemingly closed.

But surveys are blunt measures of shared phenomena. While they
are great for scaled analysis, they cannot provide a systematic account
of day-to-day life on the ground. As I observed classroom life over
the course of an academic year at each of the schools in the study, I
became acutely aware of differences in how school members talked
about the promises of digital technology and the divergent ways they
enacted the use of digital tools practice.

For example, iPads at Heathcliff were used for online communication
and collaboration, integrating photos and videos taken of friends and
family into projects, and sometimes even for adapting the assignment
to the students' own interests. At Chávez, however, such activities were
seen as valueless when compared with what were called "basic skills," or
routinized, creativity-free demonstrations of digital labor: using correct
grammar online, finding online media but not creating it, completing
prescribed digital assignments but not adapting assignments based on
students' ideas from their digital experiences.

These differences were also evident in the use of common tools. Although students at each school enjoyed playing *Minecraft*, a creativity-
centered video game, only Heathcliff students were allowed to periodically swap out a writing assignment with a video game creation. It
appeared that kids' digital play reaped different rewards depending on
the school. Young people's digital creativity—the innovative potential
so celebrated by contemporary stories of twenty-first-century success—
was *required* by teachers at Heathcliff and *dismissed* at Chávez.

What gives? Digital technologies were certainly woven into the fabric of each of the middle schools in this study, but scholars caution us against assuming that iPads, laptops, and other devices have power in and of themselves over the particulars of day-to-day life. In fact, although each school had many similar technologies at their disposal and depended on them for instruction, they perceived their uses in very different ways. This stands in contrast to what some call "technological determinism," or the idea that the very existence of technologies exerts a structuring influence.[1] This line of thinking paints technology as uniformly either *the solution* or *the barrier* to achievement gaps in schools, rather than considering how technologies are adopted in different ways and why.

In the 1980s and 1990s, schools rolled out early computers for teaching.[2] Education researchers and popular media reported that the presence of these devices had an inherent impact on the classroom, without respect to human factors that shaped how they were adopted. The teachers and administrators at the schools in this study exhibited a similar, shared rhetoric around digital technology use at school: digital technologies must be integrated in the classroom no matter what; students need digital skills to succeed in school; and digital know-how will surely help students succeed in the twenty-first-century economy.

Here, sociologists may have the explanatory upper hand in understanding why technologies may be used differently in different schools. There may be institutional factors at play that structure differentiated instructional approaches. One common argument is that children arrive at school with unequal sets of advantages, like a leg up on certain skills, given to them by their families of origin. I explore this in depth in the next chapter, countering that nearly all youth in the study shared baseline sets of digital skills (a fascinating artifact of youth-led digital adoption nationwide) and that these similar skills were still treated differently by schools. Another sociological body of work that I explore here focuses on the powerful role that institutions play in constructing social reality for their inhabitants.[3] Social reproduction theorists argue that schools differently impose informal sets of expectations on students in ways that reproduce class-based inequality. They argue that teachers collectively share beliefs about the labor market prospects of their student population and then enact these beliefs during instruction through "discipline." The term applies not simply to correcting students' bad behavior, but to an institutional process of socialization that determines appropriate behavior and internalizes norms in students.[4]

Social reproduction theory takes a Marxist stand on how children's creativity is controlled and cultivated in ways that lead to divergent labor market outcomes. Discipline, in this sense, is the means by which the "threatening" potential of kids' creativity—the extent to which they are allowed to have new ideas that could meaningfully change classroom life—is controlled. Research shows that teachers systematically limit the potential of youth of color by devaluing the cultural forms they bring to school because they are not well aligned with normative expectations. In one study, Angela Valenzuela finds that signs of students' Mexican-influenced culture, including Spanish language, Spanish-sounding names, and approaches to learning favored by Mexican schools, are deemed useless for achievement at schools in the United States.[5] In another study, Prudence Carter similarly finds that the cultural styles and interests of working-class Black and Latinx students are devalued by teachers at their schools.[6] As a result, these children take on the burden of adapting, with mixed success, to White middle-class institutional expectations that have little to do with their potential as learners. And in yet another example, a study by Patricia M. McDonough finds that guidance counselors advise working-class high schoolers to apply for working-class jobs, whereas they coach middle- and upper-class high schoolers to apply to colleges.[7] Teachers' instructional practices are thus shaped by a collective "common sense" about their students and their potential. This logic may shape the perceived value and uses of similar technologies depending on the school's student population.

It thus becomes the ethnographic task to document this "common sense" at each middle school and connect these varied logics with instructional practice. How do teachers construct the value of digital technologies? How, if at all, are digital technologies used in patterned ways by schools?

THREE MIDDLE SCHOOLS

Social reproduction theorists have fielded a series of critiques over the years, many of them well warranted. As a direct extension of Marxist thinking, much related work for many years focused almost exclusively on social class and the unequal distribution of wealth. Contemporary work is more illustrative of the ways in which schools inadvertently assemble a *matrix* of domination, in which statuses such as race-ethnicity, gender, sexuality, disability, etc., are profoundly linked to the school processes that set children up for unequal labor market outcomes. In this book, I largely focus on the intersection of race-ethnicity and social class in an effort to do some justice to these literatures. I periodically allude to, but do not well develop, how gender is inflected in the cases I study. Gender, sexuality, and other intersections are critical factors in need of unpacking to fully explore digital education and inequality. I humbly turn to my colleagues to help address these gaps.

One of the central benefits of comparative ethnographic research is that I am able to chart the challenges and opportunities of using digital technology in schools where I could account for many of the factors that are said to shape technology use. I specifically selected schools where education technologies were widely available and where administrators were committed to financially and programmatically supporting technology use in the classroom. Teachers also exhibited a comparable spectrum of training and stated technology skill at each school (see the appendix for more detail on teacher characteristics). I was also fortunate that at the time of my study, teachers even reported that standardized testing was not a constraining factor. California was undergoing a rollout of new digitized testing, and teachers said that this rollout was a calibration period and they could not be expected to prepare their students for an exam nobody had seen before.

Another methodological contribution I add here to studies of education and technology is that although each school in this study shares similar commitments to technology in the classroom, the student populations vary by student race-ethnicity and social class (see table 2.1). Heathcliff Academy is a private middle school with a predominant population of wealthy, White youth. Sheldon Junior High is a public middle school whose student body is composed largely of middle-class Asian American youth. And César Chávez Middle School is a public middle school serving primarily working-class Latinx youth. These differences allow me to unearth when and why student race-ethnicity and class matter in shaping different constructions and uses of digital technology at school.

Despite similarities in school digital access and training, and despite the general lack of state test pressure, digital tools were used in different ways to different ends. As I discuss in this chapter and throughout the book, social forces undergird the patterned yet disparate uses of similar technologies available at school. At schools with similar technology availability, similar institutional commitment to technology integration, and similar teacher training, the norms and habits ingrained in each school differently establish webs of meaning associated with the value of digital technology. The different student racial-ethnic and class populations in this study thus experience quite different educational experiences with very similar digital tools.

TECHNOLOGY TALK: DIGITAL TECHNOLOGY AND EDUCATIONAL PROMISE

During my first interviews with teachers, I asked what they thought about the role of technology in schooling. "Just look at Salman Khan—ugh, I'm obsessed!" said Ms. Fillion, a sixth-grade math teacher at Chávez. "He's revolutionized learning. Technology is the key to getting these kids into good schools and jobs someday."

Khan Academy was all the rage among the teachers in my study at the time that I began fieldwork. Salman Khan founded the nonprofit organization in 2006 to develop tutorial videos aimed at helping primary school students get "unstuck" during common school assignments in subjects like math or science. His name frequently came up when I asked teachers about the value of technology with respect to schooling. "I mean, it goes without saying that we use Khan Academy whenever we can," explained Ms. Leary, a sixth-grade language arts teacher at Sheldon Junior High. "Teachers only know so much, and it's a good way for kids to learn on their own and take it to the next level. *That's* what prepares them for the future."

Teachers at each school cited Khan and his work as an example of the promise of technology for improving education. "We actually had Salman come speak here, you know," said Ms. Kramer, an eighth-grade science teacher at Heathcliff. I learned that the school recently got the CEO of Khan Academy to speak to teachers and students about the power of technology for learning. "He was so amazing. These things available online help us and these kids move in the right direction."

The promise of digital tools for learning carried considerable weight not only among teachers but also in both education reforms and research on digital literacies. As schools increasingly get access to digital technologies for learning, researchers have focused on the importance of teaching students digital skills to find information online so that they can learn at their own, individualized pace. Teachers across all three schools drew upon a triple mythos of the importance of digital technologies for learning: that integrating technologies into regular classroom practice was good no matter what; that digital tools were essential to a pedagogy that leads to positive academic outcomes; and that digital tools were essential to improving students' odds of getting a job in the twenty-first century. Khan Academy was seen by teachers as one digital means by which to help kids achieve some of these educational goals, and Salman himself was regarded as an inspiration to teachers and their students.

When reflecting on the role of technology in the classroom, teachers at each school shared that they believed that it was necessary for digital technologies to be integrated to give students a proper education. "I've worked in schools where there's one computer from the nineties in each classroom and it sits in the corner and never gets used," said Ms. McDonough, a seventh-grade language arts teacher at Sheldon. "I mean, how embarrassing! Technology must be *integrated* to be effective; it should be a part of how you teach each lesson." Faculty emphasized that technology should be integrated with learning, meaning that technologies should be woven into their everyday practices. "Every subject, every day," Mr. Filippo, a seventh-grade social studies teacher at Heathcliff, put it bluntly. "For teaching to be effective, and for technology to be effective, it has to be built into our lessons. That's how technology can do what it's supposed to, to help these kids." By including it somehow in their lessons, and doing it regularly, teachers could ensure that technology would achieve its full effect in helping students learn. "I mean, think about all the ways we use technology in our daily lives. Why should school be excluded from that?" asked Ms. Underwood, an eighth-grade math teacher at Chávez. "In today's age, for school to be good for kids, you need to include technology just like we do everywhere else." Faculty at each school constructed the value of technology as essential for schooling.

One reason why teachers saw digital technology integration as essential was that it helped from a pedagogical point of view. Faculty argued that digital technologies were necessary to good teaching practice for nearly every academic subject. "Oh my gosh, don't even get me started," said Ms. Ullman, a seventh-grade history teacher at Sheldon. "There are *tons* of ways digital skills help with learning history. I mean, these days you have to know how to Google to look up and learning about anything—like the Persian War." Ms. Ullman, and other teachers across a variety of subjects, described the power of using the internet to supplement their instruction. "Personalized learning is also really important, and technology has really helped with that," explained Mr. Hagan, a sixth-grade science teacher at Chávez. "We have software or websites that let us give assignments that are at the level that the student is at. We can know right away how they're doing and make sure they're challenged." When asked about the value of digital technology for schooling, many teachers at each school talked about personalized learning, or the notion that students have individual learning needs that should be attended to in order to help them achieve. "I mean, personalized learning has always been a thing," explained Mr. Crump, an eighth-grade language arts teacher at Sheldon. "But just think. Never before have we had the tools to not only know our students' performance at any time, but also then provide them with new challenges tailored to their level. Technology lets us do that."

Teachers also shared a vision that digital technology was essential for helping their students eventually succeed in the labor market. "It's honestly a sin that there are still schools out there without things like iPads or laptops or SMART boards," explained Ms. West, a sixth-grade science teacher at Sheldon. "We know that having technology around helps kids learn and helps them in the future. If we know that, why aren't we making sure it's our number one priority everywhere?"

Ms. Grey, a sixth-grade language arts teacher at Chávez, expressed a similar complaint. "It honestly breaks my heart that there are kids out there who will go through their entire education never having used a computer," she lamented. "It's as if our country has decided to send those kids directly to the streets." Teachers at each school exhibited a shared philosophy that digital technologies should be included as part of the fabric of classroom life to help students achieve. "Our country should be ashamed of themselves," scolded Ms. Leary, a sixth-grade language arts teacher at Sheldon. "More schools should have the digital technology that we do. These kids need it if they want a shot at a good future." When first sharing this belief, teachers typically drew upon a moral obligation to provide and integrate technology at school. In their view, providing educational technologies at school was directly associated with improved academic outcomes and avoiding students' later failures in the labor market.

Teachers at each school exhibited a shared language around the stated value of technology at school. They believed digital technology was essential to learning, that it should be integrated in most lessons, that it was an important part of a successful pedagogical approach, and that it was morally important insofar as it would help their students get jobs someday. These views resonate closely with what existing scholarship has called *technological determinism,* or the notion that technologies in and of themselves will effect particular outcomes by their presence—that by being integrated they will help students learn; that they make learning more personalized; that they lead to better labor market outcomes. But how did teachers use digital technology in practice?

PORTALS AT HEATHCLIFF ACADEMY
(primarily wealthy and White students)

Heathcliff, like the other schools in this study, had a wide assortment of digital tools for learning. But faculty and staff exhibited much more complex perceptions of digital tools when reflecting on their particular student population of predominately wealthy, White students. Reflecting on the school's 1-to-1 iPad rollout, Mr. Crouse, the school technology lab manager, explained to me how ideal uses of technology for education form a bridge between students' lives and school:

> The iPad is not really a device—it's a portal. What you need is for every student to have a portal into web-based solutions. It's their textbook, their agenda, a notebook, a research tool, and a camera into their lives. It's all those things. 1-to-1 isn't about just handing someone a computer. It's creating a portal to school.

This "portal" metaphor was prevalent among faculty at Heathcliff. It positioned digital objects as productive windows into students' lives. The 1-to-1 iPad program first went into effect during the year I observed and was widely supported by parents and teachers.

During classroom observation, I found that students were actively encouraged to use their iPads for note-taking, calendaring, communications with faculty and their peers, and as a multimedia recorder. Students periodically held their iPads up to take pictures of notes on the whiteboard or in handouts. Teachers also regularly created classroom activities that required students to take photos of something at school or at home to be included in their presentation. For example, Ms. Richards assigned her eighth-grade science class to take photographs of a substance to illustrate an element from the periodic table. Ms. Ross required her art class students to take photos of their creations for their own portfolio. Faculty encouraged students to use their iPads to create and share their own media for school assignments. Like faculty at other schools, Heathcliff teachers saw digital technology as essential for learning. But Heathcliff faculty saw technologies as portals into kids' lives at home and among peers, and such a construction encouraged students to regularly create and share media from their home lives as part of effective teaching.

Heathcliff also required students to use software on their iPads that facilitated frequent links between students' work and the cloud, an online environment where faculty could observe and engage with students' digitally mediated activities. Using a combination of Google Drive and a file management application, teachers created folders and files within Google Drive and distributed them to students. Students would then create their own text, spreadsheet, or presentation documents, and teachers would observe their work in real time to leave comments. "It's fabulous because I can see all the great work that they're doing either in school or at home," said Ms. Pryce, reflecting on using Drive for her English classes. "They're used to teachers popping in on their assignments while they're working from wherever. I think they like knowing we're around and there to help. And I like knowing they're doing their work!" Faculty also used cloud-based apps to facilitate group projects, where students would work collaboratively on a project, like a writing assignment, together. This approach to iPads fostered regular interactions and a sense of connectedness between students and teachers in day-to-day school life. Integrating technology at Heathcliff included peer-to-peer sharing between students and faculty as part of a learning process.

During the time of my fieldwork, major academic textbook publishers were transitioning to electronic textbooks that provide an interactive, multimodal learning experience for students. Like the other schools in this study, Heathcliff purchased these textbooks for their classrooms. Faculty at the school did, at times, struggle with adapting to the e-textbook and learning its various features, but I found that they would learn with and from students who figured out how to use them. For example, Mrs. Lawson, a sixth-grade history teacher, was using an e-textbook to teach students about manifest destiny. As I peered over onto students' iPads, I saw them scrolling through a combination of text descriptions about the history of manifest destiny and animated diagrams illustrating the concept and even playing narrated videos about the topic. Students also actively used note-taking features within the textbook to annotate parts of the document for later reference. During class, faculty encouraged students to use these multimodal features of the textbook on their iPad for playing games, watching videos, and taking notes—all within the e-book.

Teachers also used interactive whiteboards in ways that supported the school's "portal" approach to digital technology. All but one class-room were equipped with a touch-responsive computerized screen. Using special markers, teachers took notes on the board that could be stored as a file and sent to students for reference. Mr. Filippo, a seventh-grade social studies teacher, saved his whiteboard mark-ings when lecturing for both his students and his own purposes. "It helps the students keep track of what we talked about," he explained. "And it helps me remember what on earth I talked about then, too!" Teachers regularly invited students up to the interactive whiteboard to solve math problems, play learning games, or give presentations. Ms. Kaufman allowed students to mirror their iPad screens to the whiteboard for classroom activities. During one lesson on using com-mands in Spanish, she divided the class up into teams and asked one student from each team to collect answers on their iPad and mir-ror them to the class. Incidentally, as a student tried to mirror their screen, they accidentally shared it to the screen in a neighboring class-room. We could hear laughter through the wall. Students and fac-ulty regularly used digital technologies like interactive whiteboards for collaboration and sharing as part of classroom activities. These technologies were used in ways that created permeable boundaries between members of the school.

A software application used by all three schools in this study was online grade-reporting software. This software is designed to allow teachers to enter students' grades from homework assignments, pro-jects, quizzes, and tests, and also leave comments on the grades, then distribute them to students and parents in real time. However, only Heathcliff faculty used this software as a portal to actively connect teachers, parents, and students to real-time reports of students' edu-cational progress. "I can add Bobby's grade right here and when I click 'submit' it goes live to *everyone*," said Ms. Lawson, a sixth-grade history teacher. "Parents can even set it so that if their kid's updated grades are below, like, a B, then they get an email notification." Al-though teachers periodically lamented that their students and their families were too grade-oriented, they nonetheless treated technolo-gies like grade-reporting software and the interactive whiteboard as portals to connect participants across the school ecology. The real-time grades enabled students to start conversations with faculty about how to improve their work. "It's kinda cool because it shows you the grade, and if you are worried about it you can message the teacher," said Cordelia, an eighth-grade student at Heathcliff. "I messaged my English teacher after a really bad quiz grade went up. She met with me to go over the quiz, it helped a lot." Platforms like the grading system were used to connect students and their families with teachers over students' performance, creating efficient ways for students to improve their work.

While all three schools in this study used 1-to-1 devices and online software for learning, Heathcliff's use of *creative* software far surpassed the others'. Students had access to the latest Adobe creative suites, including Dreamweaver, Illustrator, and Photoshop. They also benefited from video creation software like iMovie and Final Cut Pro for activities designed to promote students' creative production, where students were encouraged to mess around with the software to make something fun. "These kids often have these hobbies and they do them at home," said Mr. Crouse as he explained their approach to digital production. "But we in school are in the business of helping kids find passion for it that they may not have known they had. We use these tools to help take their interests to the next level." I learned from teachers and students that youth did make lots of things at school, like wire interesting light patterns with Arduino kits or even create their own video games using software at school. Faculty enabled students to use software for creative purposes and validated them for their creations.

Heathcliff faculty's use of digital technologies actively connected members of the school ecology, including teachers, students, and their families. This "portal" approach to technology resonated with how they used iPads, interactive whiteboards, cloud-based applications, and even grading software. Moreover, the school used creative software to encourage youth to become "makers," bridging their own interests with the school setting. These practices stood in contrast to how the other schools imagined the value of technology for school. As I discuss next, faculty at Sheldon Junior High conceived of openly networked spaces online as a means for top-down supervision and scrutiny.

SURVEILLANCE AT SHELDON JUNIOR HIGH
(primarily middle-class Asian American students)

Mr. O'Gavahan, the principal at Sheldon Junior High, asked that I attend a faculty meeting to be introduced on my first day observing at the school. At Sheldon, faculty meetings were held at desks in the school library, which occupied a central and very public region of the main building on campus. The seating area fit about fifty people at tables and connected to the library computer lab, which held about thirty computers. The "walls" surrounding the seating area and lab were bookshelves about six feet high; the perimeter just above was a substantial walkway all around connecting classrooms and the main entrance of the building. As we convened, staff and students passing by could listen in on the meeting. Some youth often did during the meetings that I attended, leering over from above and watching the action.

I later learned that the school was structured more broadly to accommodate this "open-door" approach to teaching. Most classrooms did not have doors, and some were missing walls altogether. The exception was the newest building at the far end of campus, which was built around a very open and nicely landscaped quad. It boasted eight rooms for eighth-grade classes. However, even these rooms were connected in pairs by ten-foot-wide sliding glass doors. "It's kind of hard to teach sometimes when anyone can walk in and interrupt your lesson," said Mr. Bagby, a seventh-grade social studies teacher. "But it's good because we can all help keep an eye on each other's students." Like teachers at Heathcliff and Chávez, Sheldon teachers saw integrating digital technologies as essential for good teaching. But in practice, they constructed the value of a digitally integrated school quite differently. At Sheldon, openness and transparency were synonymous with surveillance. Faculty demands to monitor students informed the ways they used digital technologies to teach.

Although Sheldon did have some iPads available to faculty for teaching, the school rolled out a 1-to-1 Chromebook program for most of its classes. Chromebooks are laptops that primarily operate with an internet connection and through the cloud. Most teachers said that they loved having Chromebooks because they boot up quickly and make student login processes seamless, two issues that slowed down instruction with other types of laptops. After talking to the more tech-savvy faculty at Sheldon, I learned that cloud-only laptops had an appeal as a surveillance tool. Mr. Kenworth, an art teacher at the school, explained:

> Teachers like to say here that Chromebooks are good because they are fast. But it's more than that. The old laptops had hard drives that made it harder to tell not only when a student does something bad but who it is that's doing it. Chromebooks make everything a student does visible to us online.

Faculty at Sheldon used this monitoring to police students for various types of online behavior. I spoke with teachers and administrators who tried to keep an eye out for students texting or chatting with classmates, playing games, watching YouTube, or bypassing school online filters to access unapproved content online.

Sheldon went to great lengths to use their digital platforms to discipline and punish students for their online behavior. For example, Mr. Lenk, a technology instructor at the school, explained how students experienced this surveillance as they became accustomed to school:

> The other day there was a kid sending messages to his friend online during my class. The next day I printed out four pages, everything he typed. He was mortified. But at school we are responsible for them. Some server has recorded everything they did . . . they don't get that. There's a difference between Facebook at home and Facebook at school, and nobody tells them. They learn the hard way.

Many other faculty like Mr. Lenk used cloud-based student data as an opportunity to teach lessons about appropriate behavior online "the hard way." School wireless access was strictly guarded for this purpose. The school maintained a whitelist policy online where they blocked all content on the internet with the exception of specific websites they predetermined as safe and valuable. I myself tried to obtain access to the school wireless account to do some of my own work but had to go through a process each visit to obtain a randomized password for a guest account that would last for only twelve hours. I ultimately decided not to use their school wireless because of concerns over school surveillance and my raw data. Students were not permitted to access the school wireless unless they used it under an account tied to their name.

Unlike Heathcliff, Sheldon made a decision not to purchase any interactive whiteboards for their classrooms. "Our principal decided not to get interactive whiteboards because he didn't want teachers up at the front of the class all the time," explained Ms. West, a sixth-grade science teacher. "The expectation is that teachers should walk around students' desks as they do their work to stay on top of what they are up to." I initially thought the absence of interactive whiteboards was a financial one but instead learned that they were purposefully not purchased to support greater student surveillance. In the absence of interactive whiteboards, teachers used traditional projectors that can mirror the teacher's computer. Students rarely came up to the front of the room to present. Instead, faculty used a variety of software for quizzes, tests, and exam-like classroom activities. Teachers used Google apps, like Google Documents and Spreadsheets, but the main use of these platforms was to create gradable databases that students filled in from their Chromebooks. In other words, teachers used Chromebooks and cloud technology to replicate traditional tests.

Digital technologies at Sheldon were used in ways that constricted their openly networked design. Whereas at Heathcliff students and teachers used Google Documents for asynchronous and synchronous collaboration and feedback on writing assignments, Sheldon teachers restricted the platform's use to high-stakes, participatory engagement. "In Google Docs I can monitor what they're typing," said Mr. McNally, an eighth-grade science teacher. "I can see who has made every edit, who has contributed every word, who's being stupid." Mr. McNally, like other Sheldon teachers, used the real-time application to regulate online writing and other forms of digital production. Mr. Oruche, a sixth-grade language arts teacher, accomplished similar types of regulation by requiring students in the same Google Docs group project to grade each other. "It helps me figure out who is doing good work and who is messing around," he explained. When not using applications for group projects, teachers actively sought to disable peer communications features within the apps so that only the teacher could transmit messages.

Although Sheldon purchased electronic textbooks very similar to those used at Heathcliff, Sheldon faculty went to great lengths to use them like traditional textbooks. For example, Ms. McDonough, a seventh-grade language arts teacher, used an e-textbook to teach a lesson on Harriet Tubman as part of a related writing project. Students each had their Chromebooks open to the textbook. "Remember the two-finger rule," she said to her students. "When I walk around, you should only be using your two fingers to scroll the page to follow along as I read the book." Ms. McDonough's "two-finger rule" meant that students should not be typing or using their trackpad to explore other features of the textbook. If students were not scrolling, she would ask that they put their hands in their lap. These practices at Sheldon had the effect of capitalizing on certain features of digital technologies that conform to existing expectations of students, rather than take advantage of innovative, multimodal features like those in contemporary textbooks.

As with other digital platforms at school, Sheldon teachers used their online grading software in ways that minimized opportunities for engagement between students and their families. "I definitely wait until the very last minute to put grades online," said Mr. Crump, an eighth-grade language arts teacher. "The moment you put a grade up, you'll be getting students and parents calling you demanding why they didn't get an A. That's not how I teach." Most faculty at Sheldon explained that they used this delay tactic on grade reporting to reduce opportunities for discussing grades with students and their families. "I make it crystal clear on my website not to email me to cry about grades," said Ms. Ullman, a seventh-grade history teacher. "I give them everything they need in class about deadlines and criteria for doing well on assignments, and that's how it is." While faculty at Heathcliff used grading software to connect with students and their families about classroom assignments, Sheldon teachers took a hands-off approach to discourage similar engagement.

Sheldon faculty's use of digital technology for surveillance and "traditional" forms of schooling, like quizzes and tests, offered a stark comparison to Heathcliff, where digital technologies were seen as valuable for learning when they provided connected, participatory settings for multimodal engagement with teachers and peers. Sheldon's "open-door" style of teaching with technology thus diverged from Heathcliff's "portal" approach by creating a strict boundary around what constitutes learning with technology. We'll next see at César Chávez Middle School that some of the same digital technologies were used for teaching rote skills rather than creativity.

BASIC SKILLS AT CÉSAR CHÁVEZ MIDDLE SCHOOL
(primarily working-class Latinx students)

My first stop during fieldwork at César Chávez was at the school computer lab to attend a technology working group meeting composed of the principal and nine faculty at the school. The group was organized by Ms. Bryant, the school's technology lab manager, and Mr. Erickson, the principal, in an effort to identify their priorities for digital technology and to find ways to support faculty elsewhere at the school. "We need to create a *vision* for technology here," Mr. Erickson said to the group. "Once we have that vision, the funding will follow. But we have to figure it out first." Ms. Gellar, a sixth-grade math teacher, furrowed her brow. "We can't think of technology as an elective," she said, with force. "It needs to be *every day*. They need twenty-first century skills to get a job someday." Mr. Weber, an eighth-grade history teacher, nodded. "And we all know these kids can text and do Instagram," added Ms. Woodside. "But if we want to help them we need to teach them basic skills they'd need to survive high school and hopefully get a job someday."

As I interviewed faculty and observed day-to-day life at Chávez, I witnessed how a shared discourse around teaching "basic skills" with digital technology informed instruction. Interestingly, Chávez boasted a panoply of hardware and software almost identical to what was available for teaching at Heathcliff. There were several key factors that minimized school-level digital divides for Chávez despite the fact that it served a disadvantaged population. First, the "techie" teachers at the school actively applied for grants to purchase up-to-date equipment or brought in their own technology for instruction. Second, the principal and the technology lab manager worked closely with the district to jockey for funding to annually purchase iPad and laptop carts for the school. And third, the district hired an education technology support specialist who hopped between Chávez and another school to ensure that their technology was regularly operable. Despite the similarities in digital technology access between Heathcliff and Chávez, Chávez faculty saw the value of technology much differently—not for creative expression, but to develop rote digital skills for technical job tracks.

The school provided 1-to-1 access for their students, with half their classes using iPads and the other half using Chromebooks. But while Heathcliff's "portal" approach to technology facilitated a permeable window between kids' own lives and school, the emphasis on basic skills at Chávez rendered instruction a unidirectional experience. For example, although teachers had interactive whiteboards and devices for students, students were often instructed to consume media rather than create it. Mr. Chase, a seventh-grade science teacher, would regularly play cartoons about the basics of physics for his students that they watched idly from their seats. This stood in contrast to whiteboard use at Heathcliff, where students were regularly interacting with the whiteboard, either physically or digitally by mirroring their screens. Relatedly, when using laptops or iPads for assignments, Chávez students were encouraged to seek out new media like images, animations, or videos, but they were not provided opportunities to *create* these types of media. As I discuss in more depth in other chapters, this is because Chávez faculty did not believe that students' own creative potential online had value for working-class jobs. As teachers, they saw their role as providing the skills they believed students needed in order to do well, minimizing the digital know-how students brought with them to school.

"Basic skills" also did not include peer-to-peer communications among students, and Chávez created barriers to prevent students from interacting over digital technology. As at Sheldon, Chávez faculty used applications like Google Documents or Spreadsheets and did not permit chatting with peers online. In contrast to Sheldon, students' online communications were not seen as threatening. Rather, they were positioned as *useless*. For example, Ms. Embry, a seventh-grade language arts teacher, would use Google Documents for student writing projects. "I tell them not to chat with each other in the document," she explained to me. "It's not exactly the worst thing, it's just not going to help them at all learn how to write. It's a distraction." Teachers typically disabled peer-to-peer chat features in learning software or at the very least minimized the value of these communications for the classroom activities at hand.

Although the hardware at Chávez was similar to that available at Heathcliff, Chávez was noticeably different in that they offered next to none of the creative software platforms that Heathcliff provided. Heathcliff students also played or even created their own video games as part of a learning experience, but video games were seen as frivolous distractions at Chávez. There were only a few games used in the technology lab, including a game for learning how to type and a programming game called Scratch. This software was sanctioned because it fit with the basic skills discourse that idealized typing and programming as valuable outcomes.

Like Sheldon, Chávez used digital technology to monitor their students. In contrast, however, Chávez tracked certain types of student behavior as a means of watching out for their well-being. The school had an online portfolio application that teachers updated and shared with each other to keep abreast of students' academic development and signs of mental health. "We really care about these kids, and so we make sure to update information in case something comes up," Ms. Ramirez explained to me. "We're not really tracking these kids to punish them when they don't do well on a test, it's more so we can figure out what works best and also keep an eye out if something seems off at home." Although Chávez did not provide students with agency to communicate among themselves, teachers did use digital platforms to collaborate and share in ways they believed were in the best interests of their students. Faculty typically described their students as well-intentioned, good kids. In this vein, there were multiple wireless accounts at the school that were not password-blocked and were rarely monitored. In contrast to Sheldon's "whitelist" policy, Chávez used a "blacklist" policy online where all content, with the exception of specific websites deemed dangerous, was accessible.

At Chávez faculty used the latest digital technologies to encourage the development of skills in typing, programming, online research, and digital production like online writing. If a learning scientist were to conduct a survey at Heathcliff and Chavez, they would find similar closures of digital divides and comparable development of key digital literacies identified by education research. However, the focus on basic skills minimized students' development as creative producers. Chávez disabled creative uses of software, like most forms of digital production, including images and video. Faculty also dismissed the value of peer-to-peer communications among students online, as well as video games for learning that were valorized at Heathcliff. Faculty used digital technologies to provide top-down lessons for students that lessened the type of relational learning experienced by youth at Heathcliff.

SITUATING DIGITAL TECHNOLOGIES AT SCHOOL

Heathcliff Academy, Sheldon Junior High, and César Chávez Middle School were all examples of educational institutions that have closed digital divides at the school level. They provided a variety of up-to-date digital technologies for learning, and each included some variation of a 1-to-1 device program for their students. Faculty also all maintained that digital technology integration was essential to twenty-first-century teaching, both from a pedagogical point of view and to help students prepare for the labor market down the road. This thinking resonates with the technological determinist view that putting similar high-quality technologies in the hands of teachers and students will result in comparable outcomes. However, as I illustrate in this chapter, teachers differently constructed the value of digital technologies for teaching depending on the school. As a result, they used them differently.

At Heathcliff, faculty invoked a view of digital technologies as productive "portals" into the lives of young people, and they used iPads, interactive whiteboards, cloud-based software, and even video games to bolster students' creative potential through online collaboration and digital production. Sheldon, however, saw student uses of digital technology as potential threats; instead, they used digital technologies for surveillance and disabled the most innovative features of these platforms, preferring instead to use online software for traditional quizzes and tests. Chávez shared with Heathcliff many similar digital technologies for teaching, and their students developed comparable skills in typing, programming, and creating online documents. However, Chávez emphasized the need for "basic skills" with digital technology above all else—faculty minimized the value of using digital technologies for peer communications, video games, and creative digital production, facilitating instead a consumption-oriented learning experience.

In the next chapter, I explore how these constructions of technology pair with teachers' specific disciplinary practices with regard to children's online play. Teachers determined whether young people's digital play was valuable to school or not, either staving off or enabling play for educational achievement.

2

DISCIPLINING PLAY

While observing Mr. Oruche's sixth-grade language arts class, I noticed that a student was playing *Minecraft* on his phone. *Minecraft* is a game centered on digital creation; players can build towns and cities as part of the gameplay. The class had free work time where they were to complete a writing assignment reflecting on a story they had read about ancient civilization. But this youth had finished early. He had his phone on his lap just under his desk and played the game silently.

Typical of teachers at Sheldon Junior High, Mr. Oruche slowly patrolled the classroom to check on students' work. His eyebrows narrowed as he neared this student's desk, and he snatched the mobile device from his hands with a practiced precision. "Detention," Mr. Oruche said. He turned around to face the rest of the class. "If I have to remind anyone else that playing video games in class is off limits, then you're getting a *zero* on your assignment."

Just two days later, I was observing Mr. Filippo's seventh-grade social studies class at Heathcliff Academy. Students were similarly pursuing free work time, this time while working on an assignment incidentally also related to ancient civilizations. Most students were using their iPads to explore an e-book chapter specific to the assignment. One youth, however, was hunched over her iPad and had *Minecraft* open instead. A few other nearby students stopped what they were doing to position themselves over the shoulder of this youth and look at what she was doing.

Eventually this caught the attention of the teacher. He walked over and joined the kids looking over her shoulder. "Holy cow, what's that?" said Mr. Filippo. The student held up her phone and pointed at the screen. "Look, I tried to build the pyramid from Egypt we talked about," she explained. An onlooking youth pointed at the screen. "Wait, did you build the crypt underneath, too?" She shook her head. "Not yet, but I'm building tunnels underneath." Mr. Filippo stood up and clapped his hands to get the class's attention. "Everyone please put down your work for just a second. Angela, could you share with us what you've been working on? It's really cool and ties together what we've been studying."

Roughly 74 percent of US youth between ages thirteen and fourteen play video games, and the students in this study were no exception.[1] I often heard casual chatter among young people about video games and watched as kids tried to fit in gameplay on mobile devices while at school. But as I conducted my fieldwork, I became acutely attuned to the frequent moments where teachers evaluated not just schoolwork but their students' digital play. In these examples, both students were playing a mobile game during free work time. The student at Sheldon was penalized for gaming, whereas the student at Heathcliff was treated as if their activity was potentially valuable to learning. How does kids' play factor into day-to-day life in the classroom? Has the proliferation of digital technologies changed classroom learning at all? What explains the differences between the youth at Sheldon and Heathcliff?

One of the reasons why I chose to study human-computer interaction among youth and young adults is that they are, in the contemporary moment, among the first adopters of digital innovations that are increasingly becoming ubiquitous. Today's young people have unprecedented access to, and facility with, digital technologies. As of 2018, a whopping 95 percent of teens have access to a smartphone and a gaming console with no difference by family income or race-ethnicity.[2] Mizuko Ito and her colleagues provide the most comprehensive explication to date of what these youth are doing online. In their large-scale, comparative ethnographic study of digital youth, they find that young people use digital platforms and interactions online not as a replacement for youth culture but rather as an extension of it.[3] Through play online, young people "hang out" with their peers and "mess around" with the digital tools needed to use these online sites of engagement. In other words, to participate in youth culture today requires familiarity with digital tools, and specifically the ability to communicate online and engage in digital production. The example I shared at the beginning of this chapter was students using *Minecraft* to digitally create towns and cities—some facility with digital technologies is *required* to play.

A burgeoning literature in digital literacies showcases digital skills acquired through play as a profound opportunity to prepare children for the twenty-first century. Referring to this generation's internet-connected young adults as "digital youth," scholars reflect on kids' unprecedented access to, and facility with, digital technologies. Digital literacy researchers argue that young people learn digital skills through playful pursuits with peers.[4] Two sets of skills, in particular— online communication and digital production—are learned through many types of play online.[5] For example, kids use texting and social media apps to construct messages to one another in order to communicate. They also use image, audio, and video-editing software to share their favorite media from popular culture, or tinker with the design and programming embedded in applications online to engage in playful pursuits like video games. Although literacy scholars debate which types of digital activities can be most educational, there is little disagreement over whether digital play contributes to kids' baseline skills in the ability to communicate online and create and share online media.[6] These two sets of skills are prerequisite cornerstones to higher-level digital learning activities advocated by education reforms guiding twenty-first-century digital skills. Further, given high levels of access to digital tools among traditionally underserved populations like Black and Latinx youth, and youth from low-income families, there is an opportunity to level the playing field.[7] If play among peers leads to the development of core digital skills, it could help less privileged youth do better in school—they'd already have some of the basics down before they even got to class.

This phenomenon of kids' acquisition of digital skills through play is one that should catch the attention of sociologists studying cultural inequality in education. The predominant school of thought is that among the biggest predictors of inequality in education is that children arrive at school with unequal childhoods.[8] Decades of work, built upon theory by French sociologist Pierre Bourdieu, points to class-based differences in childrearing that help some kids in school

but not others.[9] As the story goes, wealthier families are more familiar with school expectations (shared expectations are part of what
Bourdieu terms a *social field*) and ingrain in their children sets of
habits and skills (what he terms a child's acquired *habitus*) that are
deployed by their children in school. Some of the documented examples of this include middle- and upper-class children knowing when
and how to ask for help, exhibiting particular school-valued interests,
and using language in ways that teachers see as educationally valuable. This transfer of knowledge and its recognition by teachers as a
valued resource for achievement are referred to as *cultural capital*.[10]

In an effort to cut through Bourdieu's jargon, I've tried to illustrate
this theory with the example of a financial exchange with a shopkeeper. Wealthy parents provide their children the shopkeeper's expected currency (idealized ways of demonstrating their academic
know-how). When this currency is shown, those wealthier children
get better grades. Poorer parents, who are less connected to educational institutions, are simply less able to socialize their children in
these habits. Further, this currency is scarce—and wealthy families
try to monopolize it, staying ahead of the game by looking for ways to
find it as well as new idealized forms of this currency. Thus, working-
class kids are systematically left behind in the classroom because they
lack such capital. Their parents don't have the "currency" their kids
need to demonstrate academic know-how.

In a study documenting the miraculous success of working-class
students who exhibit upper-class tastes, like interest in museums
and other high art, Paul DiMaggio argues that the solution to unequal childhoods is to redistribute knowledge.[11] If we could ensure
that working-class kids develop some of the same habits and skills as
wealthier parents provide their children, then we would see greater
cultural mobility for less privileged children. Kids' acquired digital
skills through *play* rather than from their parents presents a real
opportunity. If young people, regardless of their family origin, learn
similar valued skills in online communication and digital production,
we'd have a slightly more equal playing field. Or, to follow our previous metaphor, if we could redistribute the appropriate currency to
wealthy *and* poor children, we'd expect they'd more comparably do
well in school. Kids' digital skills learned through play are therefore

an opportunity to test this thesis of cultural mobility: if children show up at school with similar school-valued skills in online communication and digital production, does it help them achieve?

To gesture back to the earlier story about the two *Minecraft* players, I find that kids' digital play—signals of digital skills youth acquire from peers—is treated differently by teachers depending on the school and in ways that are currently not well explained by these existing theories of cultural inequality. First, it's worth noting that to locate the sole problem in parents' childrearing strategies—i.e., to say that poor families should teach their children the skills that wealthy parents do—is to misinterpret the theory. Rather, Bourdieu points to the educational *institution* as the problem: teachers evaluate their students based on standards of achievement that are most commonly exhibited by more privileged families. Although parents can socialize their children to develop particular habits and skills that may help in school, schoolteachers are ultimately the gatekeepers who assess whether those habits and skills are valuable.[12] In other words, kids may show up at school knowing how to use digital technologies, but teachers still must actively acknowledge these dispositions *as skills* (cultural capital) for achievement.

Schools treat kids' digital play in different ways, and these different approaches determine whether or not play is transformed into cultural capital for achievement. Some schools welcome young people's digital skills as valued cultural capital. Others treat play as irrelevant to, and a distraction from, the real work of learning. I've found that the best theoretical leverage for this finding rests on socialization theorists' slight twist of what we tend to mean by "discipline." The term does not simply refer to the correction of students' bad behavior but rather describes an institutional process that determines appropriate behavior and internalizes norms in students.[13]

Bowles and Gintis's examples highlight how schools implant teachers' messages in their students' self-concept (a "built-in supervisor") that reflect class-based expectations of them.[14] Teachers at schools serving working-class children prepare their students for working-class jobs; to prepare them for rote labor requires minimizing the value of anything but skills for the factory shop floor. Teachers at schools serving wealthy children prepare them for running companies; to prepare them for this work requires encouraging them to take creative risks and delegate. Teachers' ongoing communication to students in ways that shape their self-concept is a *disciplinary process*. You can probably feel the Marxist underscoring. In this view, teacher discipline is essentially a means to regulate the creative potential of children in ways that prepare them for the reality of the labor market. But these disciplinary strategies have the effect of cultural stratification: working-class kids are prepared for working-class jobs, and wealthier children are prepared for higher-income work. Social forces at school impose inequities within children's psychology before they even get a chance to demonstrate their potential.

Where I contend that the shopkeeper-teacher metaphor falls flat is in the treatment of student race-ethnicity or quite literally any other status but social class. According to existing work, we're left to assume that if both a working-class Latinx student and a working-class White youth learned the same valued cultural resources, teachers would equally reward them with good grades. But I think we suffer from a misinterpretation of how Bourdieu thinks about the standards upon which teachers evaluate their students' potential. Social fields, or the shared expectations of those working in educational institutions, have a set of rules that map to ideal sets of habits and skills expected of students. Although Bourdieu's work largely focused on how these expectations were tied to signals of social class, that is not necessarily the case: depending on the history of the institution and its outlying region, those expectations could be related to any set of habits, skills, or statuses as long as they are part of institutional authorities' shared expectations. For US scholars of cultural inequality to ignore the intertwined history of education and race-ethnicity in our assessment of social fields is a disservice to our theoretical models, to say the least.[15]

One way to begin treating race more seriously in our understanding of cultural inequality in schools is to understand how and why teachers discipline kids' play. We already have some clues as to how this might work from race and immigration scholars in education. Prudence Carter finds that the working-class Black youth in her study developed habits and skills from their families and outlying community that were systematically deemed by teachers to be of little value.[16]

As a result, these youth could succeed only if they found ways both to meet the needs and expectations of their home and peer networks and to acculturate to the White middle-class school standards. In another example, Angela Valenzuela finds that White teachers limit the potential of immigrant youth by devaluing the cultural forms they bring to school because they are not well aligned with normative expectations.[17] She finds that signs of students' Mexican-influenced culture, including Spanish language, Spanish-sounding names, and approaches to learning favored by Mexican schools, are deemed useless for achievement at schools in the United States. While these kids' habits and skills are different from those that the teachers expect, it is clear that teachers' perceptions are linked to a set of meanings about race-ethnicity and immigrant status that inform their disciplinary approach. In this example, teachers believed that to best help these children was to guide them away from Mexican-influenced practices and toward White nativist educational expectations.

I connect both this scholarship and early work on school socialization to show that teachers discipline play differently based on the race and class of their student population. Teachers link assumptions about students' racial and class statuses with perceived labor market outcomes, and then discipline play according to that imagined, yet very unequal, path. The outcome is a socialization process internalizing in children particular assumptions about the relationship between (school) work and play that differently prepares kids for using digital skills in educational institutions. Students at a school serving wealthy and White students come to understand that play is essential to work and enables them to shape their own curriculum; students at a school serving predominantly middle-class and Asian students are told that play is threatening to learning through high-stakes exams; and students at a school serving mostly working-class and Latinx children are told that play is irrelevant and more of a relief from tedious labor. Disciplining play is a mechanism by which kids' creativity is managed and variably shapes both their aspirations and habits in ways that light a path to either blue- or white-collar work.

A key focus of this chapter is to relax and build on the Bourdieuian assumption that parents' childrearing practices are the sole source of the cultural reproduction of inequality in education. I first show that the students in this study developed similar baseline digital skills in online communication and digital production from play online with peers. I then depart from existing scholarship on cultural inequality by illustrating how teachers differently discipline kids' very similar digital skills gained from play depending on the race and class of their student population.

GENERATIONAL SIMILARITIES IN DIGITAL PARTICIPATION

Consistent with existing work on digital youth, the sampled students at Heathcliff Academy, Sheldon Junior High, and César Chávez Middle School shared a similar baseline of both technology access and use of digital platforms. They pursued many of their interests online with peers. Among all interviewed students, 97.5 percent had regular access to one or more up-to-date computer or laptop, iPad, or internet-connected video game systems at home. One hundred percent of students had access to cell phones at home and at school, and among those 82.5 percent owned smartphones like iPhones or Android devices. Although I was not able to conduct representative surveys of the student body at each school, teachers at both schools conducted their own informal surveys of students and reported similar numbers.

Differences in student hardware ownership across schools were also rather small, with a few important caveats. Figure 2.1 shows that interviewed students at Chávez and Sheldon actually owned smartphones at higher rates than those at Heathcliff. Notably, only some youth at Chávez reported sharing home technologies with siblings owing to high cost. One Chávez youth I interviewed had a phone with a cracked screen and said he was "stuck with it" because of the cost of replacement. Clearly there are still differences in access and quality of available technology even at schools that are tech utopias in many senses. During interviews, Heathcliff students who did not have smartphones reported that their parents purposefully withheld smartphones from them to minimize the risk of bullying online. The few upper-class students who were not permitted smartphones align with some reports that wealthier families express more worries over

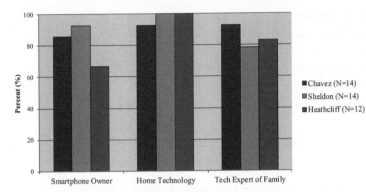

FIG. 2.1. Note: "Smartphone Owner" signifies that the student owned an internet-connected iPhone or Android device, "Home Technology" refers to student report of digital technology available at home (iPad, computer/laptop, internet-connected video game system), and "Tech Expert of Family" describes students who reported being more skilled at digital technology use than their parents or guardians.

digital technology access and their child's privacy than do working-class families.[18] As I discuss, however, these differences did not appear to shape the acquisition of basic digital skills in online communication and digital production from play online.

Interviewed students also said that they were primarily the technology experts of the family and did not learn how to use digital technologies from their parents. Eighty-five percent of all students said they were the tech experts, and slightly more students at Chávez said so than students at other schools (figure 2.1). When asked about their digital expertise relative to their families, students often laughed and asserted that their parents knew very little about technology. For example, Daniel (15 years old, Asian), a student at Sheldon, said, "I'm the techie of the family. My dad is good but I'm better." Maggie (13 years old, White), a Heathcliff student, argued that she was better at technology than her mother and father, too: "I know how to use programs that my parents don't even know how to use." And at Chávez, Bailey (14 years old, Latinx) said that she and her older brother were both skilled. "He and I are both the tech experts of the family," she said. "We fix computers and programs together." Students at each of the schools were by and large more "techie" than their parents or guardians, and indicated that they were not taught digital skills by their parents. Instead, they indicated that they developed a number of digital skills through their youth cultures.

DIGITALLY MEDIATED PLAY AMONG PEERS

Students nearly all developed digital facility through playful pursuits with peers. The kinds of online activities they participated in and skills with digital technology they developed are consistent with those described in existing work on digital youth culture. I found that youth enjoy communication through social media and digital production. In what follows, I provide examples of these activities from students at each school to illustrate the generational similarities in digital youth culture.

Nearly all sampled students at each school used some kind of social media to share text, image, and video-based communications with their peers. "I use Kik[19] and Instagram[20] on my phone," said Anthony (13 years old, Latinx), a student at Chávez. "I talk with my friends and keep up with what they're doing on my phone." Cordelia (14 years old, White), a student at Heathcliff, was an avid social media user: "I use Instagram and Snapchat[21] mostly. I *love* Snapchat, and texting. It's how I stay in touch with my friends." Andrew (13 years old, Latinx), a student at Sheldon, also used Instagram and Snapchat. "I use Instagram and Snapchat almost every day," he said. "Sometimes we record silly videos of ourselves and send them to each other." Students used social media to send messages using a variety of new media, including text, image, and video content that they developed using their phones or other hardware at home. But they also used social applications to set up activities. For example, Anne (15 years old, Asian), another student at Sheldon, used social media to keep up with her friends and coordinate hanging out. "My friends use texting and other apps like Kik to plan things and hang out in person, too." Consistent with studies of digital youth that find generational differences in digital participation, youth at all three schools used texting and other media-rich communications applications to "hang out" with friends and participate in their peer cultures. These practices also help the development of digital skills like facility with digital platforms and online communication.[22]

The second type of digital activity that students at each school pursued with their friends was digital production. Although social media use does, indeed, require that youth develop their ability to communicate across digital platforms, digital production demands considerably more technical knowledge. For example, Maggie (13 years old, White) paired up with a friend of hers at Heathcliff to write collaborative fiction online:

> My friend and I were writing for National Writing Month. We used Google Drive! We did it on Google Docs and did it chapter by chapter. One of us would do one chapter, another would do another. It was weird but it worked . . . we ended up finishing!

Maggie, with her friend, used digital tools to write stories collaboratively, peer edit, and submit to a national competition.[23] Another form of creative production is software development through computer programming. Several youth "jailbroke"[24] their mobile phones, or tweaked the phone's functionality, to program their own applications. "I jailbreak my iPod, and I tinker with it a bit," said Daniel (15 years old, Asian), a student at Sheldon. "I get into the back end of the programming. Nobody really knows I do that." Hacking and remaking parts of one's own phone requires knowledge of software programming. Danny (13 years old, Latinx), a Chávez student, also hacked some of his video games to accomplish specific goals. "When I want to get money on a game, sometimes I will mod it," he said. "You download this APK[25] stuff so the game gets tricked into giving you money. It might help me someday if I want to become a hacker! Ha. Or maybe a programmer, who knows." Students' digital production activities, including online writing and hacking, are among the most popularly idealized digital skills in research on new literacies.

Digital production does not need to be quite as technical as jailbreaking, and students at each school used image and video editing for creative purposes, as well. Sarah (15 years old, Asian), a student at Sheldon, liked creating and sharing artistic pictures she took on social media with her friends: "I think social media is super creative. If you want to learn how to do it, that is. I had to figure out how to download the right photo-editing apps to get the pictures how I wanted before I shared it on Instagram." Nathan (14 years old, White), a student at Heathcliff, said that he liked to make short videos that he uploaded on an app called Vine.[26] "Me and my friends will record each other to make little short stories that we think are funny," he said. "We'll upload them on Vine, which is like an Instagram just for video. We're trying to get more followers, but we like what we've made so far." Richard (14 years old, Latinx), a student at Chávez, produced music with his friend. Some students also pursued design-oriented games, like Armin (14 years old, Latinx), a Sheldon student, who spent a lot of time playing world-creation games. "I like building games like *Minecraft* where you can build whatever you want," he said. "I feel like I'm developing the architecture for what houses would look like in real life, or even bridges." These digital skills align with those described in scholarship on new literacies, including computer programming and design, and editing and producing media like audio, images, and videos.

Although some digital divides likely exist, the students in this study mirror national patterns in digital access and share a baseline set of digital skills that they developed mainly through their youth cultures. In what follows, I illustrate what happens when students bring these digital youth cultural practices into school. Even though teachers themselves were often less skilled with digital technology than their students, they disciplined students' digital skills in distinct ways that variably enabled their digital play as cultural capital for achievement.

THE NEXT STEVE JOBS AT HEATHCLIFF ACADEMY

Although teachers at each of the schools typically described themselves as less skilled with technology than their students, teachers perceived the value of students' digital skills differently by school. At Heathcliff, teachers saw students' own interests online as valuable, if not essential, to academic achievement. Mr. Crouse, the school technology lab manager and technology integrationist, said that ideal uses of technology formed a bridge between students' lives and school:

I always use the example of Steve Jobs going to his garage and tinkering around. Why can't the garage be at school? There's value in having school be a place where kids can come in, bring what they know from their own lives, and have their eyes light up with possibility and say, okay, I see maybe something I can do here and I can become passionate about.

Mr. Crouse saw students' "garages," or the kinds of activities they do outside, as an important part of learning. Thus, integrating these practices with schooling was the way to cultivate the next Steve Jobs—a digital version of what school socialization theory gestures to as a key mechanism that drives disciplinary processes for wealthy students. In thinking about how these labor market assumptions shape digital tool use in class, recall that teachers at Heathcliff imagined technologies for learning through a "portal" approach. Describing iPad use at school, Mr. Crouse said that iPads were "their textbook, their agenda, a notebook, a research tool, and a camera into their lives . . . 1-to-1 isn't about just handing someone a computer. It's creating a portal to school." Typically, 1-to-1 refers to a kind of education reform where each student is provided with a technology for learning, like a laptop or an iPad, but here Mr. Crouse described the reform rather as a "portal" for engagement. This portal metaphor operated at Heathcliff as a translational device for teachers to actively recognize and integrate students' digital forms as valuable cultural capital for learning at school.

Other teachers at Heathcliff also adopted this "portal" approach that blurred digital play and school. They repeatedly asserted that their students brought with them to class many useful technology skills. Mrs. Kaufman, a sixth-grade Spanish teacher at Heathcliff, said that students picked up iPad use in class very quickly: "It was seamless. I said, 'abran sus libros en el iPad a la pagina cincuenta' (open your books on the iPad to page 50). The students just did it, no problem. It's like they already know how to do everything because they play around with this stuff with their friends." Mrs. Lawson, a sixth-grade history teacher, also acknowledged that students had technical facilities that came from their digital play. "These kids are in a technology age, it's just their typical way to communicate. They love iMovie[27] and they come up with amazing videos on their own for class. Most of them are comfortable with that." Teachers described their students as already proficient in uses of technology as a result of their peer-driven participation online. At Heathcliff, faculty seemed to subscribe to the view that the digital skills acquired from hanging out with friends online have potential for learning. Teachers saw connections between students' digital skills and school-based learning.

Heathcliff teachers also described trying to integrate digital play into their instructional philosophies and practices as part of a learning agenda. Ms. Pryce, an eighth-grade language arts teacher, argued that she and her students mixed their different skill sets to create a productive learning experience. "Oh yes, they are tech savvy, just like that term 'digital native,'" she said. "They're raised with these technologies and so they are definitely good at using them at school. But it's my job as the old fogey 'digital immigrant' to take what they know and help them here." Ms. Pryce used the terms "digital native" and "digital immigrant" to position her students as budding technologists and herself as an integrationist of digital play in school. Mrs. Cramer, a seventh-grade science teacher, commented on how games that students play can be productive for school, too. "They're comfortable with many of the apps and programs they are used to, and that can really help with school. I use a lot of games, like, we have one game a student found to memorize the periodic table. I say why not?" Teachers like Mrs. Cramer saw the value of video games for learning. She encouraged youth to find ways to blend these practices during science classes. Heathcliff's art teacher, Ms. Kober, reflected on how students create art projects that get connected through social media. "One of my students had this little surfer guy he made out of clay and was using his phone to create a stop-motion claymation video and then put it on Instagram to share with his friends. They all got a kick out of it. He was doing something creative and wanted to share it, which I think is a big part of doing art." For Ms. Kober, student uses of technology bridged the divide between school activities and digital play for a more engaged learning experience. Heathcliff teachers thus had a disciplinary orientation to play that positioned their students' digital play as valuable capital for achievement.

Teachers at Heathcliff demanded that students practice integrating their digital forms and ideas at school, thus carving a path to transforming digital play into capital for learning. As part of their training at the school, students were required to "tell their story" through the use of digital technologies before an audience of their peers, who then asked them questions. In interviews, teachers joked that when students first started out doing this ritual during their first year, they were so nervous that they, in the words of Mrs. Lawson, "stand up in front of the interactive whiteboard and cry as they talk about their family dog." Over time, however, students became comfortable talking about themselves in class and before their peers and instructors. Scholarship on school socialization tends to ignore how elite students' habits and skills are cultivated by school processes, with few exceptions. What I find here echoes early suggestions that schools socialize wealthy students for Steve Jobs-esque work through a disciplinary approach to play. I essentially observed a process of legitimation, as students were required to develop comfort and facility with their own digital play and to see it as relevant and important to the school setting.

In one such class, I observed sixth-graders "telling their story" to their peers and instructors. As part of an assignment that integrated language arts, art, and technology, students were presenting a project that required them to design a PowerPoint presentation about themselves. They were required to take pictures or video outside of class, with their family or with friends, and creatively integrate this new media into the presentation. "Jessica, you're up!" said Ms. Kober. A young woman, hands at her sides, sheepishly got up out of her seat and scooted to the front of the room with a USB stick in her hand. She plugged the portable drive into the computer connected to a projector screen in the front of the room, and within moments a slide covered the wall with a picture she had taken of her family. She added images she found from the internet to the perimeter of the slide, including a photo of cats and a softball. "Hi everyone, I'm Jessica, and I this is my mom, my dad, and me," she murmured. "Jessica, you're doing great but be sure to speak up," said Ms. Kober. Jessica tapped the screen to move to the next slide and tried to speak a little louder: "One of my favorite things to do is play softball!" She tapped the screen once more, and images of a baseball and baseball bat appeared and began to animate. The baseball swung and hit the ball, and it flew across the screen. A student raised their hand: "How did you make the ball move like that!?" Jessica smiled. "I figured out that you can have two pictures on the slide do different things, so I made the baseball picture swing by itself and then made the ball move on its own once it got hit." At Heathcliff, students were required to practice creating their own online media and tinkering with the tools to edit and design assignments for class. Heathcliff constructed many learning activities as successful if they blurred the lines between students' interests and schooling.

In addition to structuring lessons that facilitated students' own creative production and collaboration at school, Heathcliff also provided students with opportunities to integrate their own digital forms into the character and image of the institution. For example, students were giving presentations at the beginning of Ms. Kramer's eighth-grade science class for a project about environmental awareness. Jimmy was at the front of the screen presenting a video he had produced on the topic. In the video, Jimmy combined multiple forms of media that included his own video recordings of his peers, as well as preexisting video created by the school administration, to talk about environmental awareness. As part of his video-editing process, he blended together video snippets of a prerecorded speech by the school principal (downloaded from the school website) with his own recordings of his friends parading around campus picking up waste for recycling. He added a popular song as background music and included titles showing the names of the actors that animated across the screen when those people appeared. I later learned that the school decided to make Jimmy's video part of the promotional material for the school since it got more attention than their other formal productions. Teachers at Heathcliff not only transformed their students' digital skills into valued capital for achievement but encouraged students to take the reins over *what counted* as achievement. Jimmy's video, which remixed school and digital play together to create something new, became a representation of the school.

Teachers' orientations to students' digital play differed by school. At Heathcliff, teachers disciplined play by integrating students' digital culture into the learning agenda. This outcome differs from classic social reproduction theories in that these privileged students were not simply being trained to maintain the "norms of the enterprise."[28] Rather, students were helping shape the norms for learning in the digital age, as evidenced in Jimmy's video example. The less digitally adept teachers benefited from students' digital skills by disciplining play in this way, allowing the institution to adapt to the digital age.

RISKY HACKERS AT SHELDON JUNIOR HIGH

Whereas at Heathcliff, students' digital forms were turned into valued capital for achievement, at Sheldon teachers actively policed the boundary between digital play and school. They perceived students' digital forms as serious threats to learning. While race was not a salient marker during interviews or observation among Heathcliff's majority-White faculty and student body, race- and class-inflected assumptions were top-of-mind for faculty at Sheldon. Teachers' orientation to students' digital play came from shared perceptions that their middle-class Asian American students were cutthroat overachievers. Those perceptions seem to be associated with a discipline-heavy approach to digital technology that positioned students' digital skills as giving them an unfair advantage over one another. As a consequence, teachers used digital technologies only for high-stakes activities and traditional exams and did not teach digital skills in online communication and digital production.

Teachers at Sheldon Junior High drew upon class- and race-based stereotypes to construct their students as risky hackers who needed discipline. They believed that their students were smart and naturally good with technology because they were Asian but also that they posed threats because competitive "Tiger Moms" had raised them. Ms. Nisbett, a seventh-grade science teacher, explained:

> I feel bad for our kids here. They grow up with a Tiger Mom culture and are taught from a young age to only get A's or they have failed. It's terrible. But it makes it hard for us as teachers because they're taught to do anything to do well, and that's not fair to other students.

Racialized depictions of their students were widely available, and I unpack the source of these stereotypes—*why* teachers discipline play—in the next chapter. Here I focus on *how* teachers actually discipline children's activities in school as a result of these stereotypes. Like Ms. Nisbett, Mr. McNally expressed frustration that his eighth-grade students had been raised to be so test-focused. "They're only as good as how they are on a test," he said. "In Asian culture, their livelihoods are about tests. The benchmark in China is about tests. We're creating people who can't think or can't problem solve, but they're good at tests."

At Sheldon Junior High, teachers described how parents pressured their children to do well in school, but I found no differences in the content of the requests by similarly aggressive parents at Heathcliff. While Heathcliff teachers imagined each of their students as the next Steve Jobs, the shared imaginary of students at Sheldon relied on racialized stereotypes of Asian students as upwardly mobile and cutthroat individuals who are intelligent and college-driven but who are also potential threats. Digital proficiency was seen as making Asian students threatening. While research suggests that teachers construct Asian students as model minorities with inherent orientations to success, I find that digital play here was perceived as giving them an unfair advantage.

Teachers at Sheldon not only doubted the value of digital skills that came from students' play. They also saw those skills as threatening to successful schooling. Ms. Ullman, a seventh-grade history teacher, believed that social media was frivolous and a distraction from learning. "Twitter doesn't help them with tests. Facebook doesn't help them with essays. It prevents them from focusing on important tasks in class and on homework," she said. "They can text, but can they type in MLA format? No." Teachers also believed that students' digital play at school would lead to disruptive hacking, as in Ms. Finnerty's comments about student hackers mentioned earlier. At Sheldon, teachers positioned the activities and digital skills developed from play as distractions and risks. This stands in contrast to theories of cultural mobility that suggest that if students share similar skills, they will get ahead—while digital play was seen as valuable at Heathcliff, Sheldon faculty saw the same activities as threatening to learning. As a result, teachers instead favored traditional institutional standards and practices, including test-taking preparation, essay writing, and meeting citation standards. They framed kids' digital play as diverging from the overall educational mission.

When teachers at Sheldon reflected on their instructional practices with digital technology, they described their teaching as successful only when they were able to strictly sanction signs of digital play. Mr. Crump, an eighth-grade language arts teacher, expended considerable energy on creating lessons with technology that restricted peer-to-peer communication:

> I use Edmodo, an app that looks like Facebook where I can create a community for my students online to share assignments and grade their work. But I make it so students cannot post to other students' walls. They can't communicate with their peers at all. I put on moderator privileges where I moderate every comment, or delete every comment. If they put up a question about an assignment online, it sends me a notification that they've done it and I decide whether it gets published or not. I think it makes them more focused on the task at hand.

At Sheldon, teachers restricted almost all forms of online peer-to-peer communication and collaboration as a way to protect the integrity of schooling. Another teacher, Mr. McNally, said that he actively prevented youth in his eighth-grade science class from interacting during online assignments. "Facebook and Instagram doesn't help them with school. The school uses of technology are *traditional*," he said. "I would never embrace social media as part of a lesson. I don't want to let go of this control that I have because then I have to monitor more and more of this garbage. I don't want to deal with all of that." Teachers at Sheldon constructed their curriculum in ways that separated digital play from school and forcefully withdrew digital play from learning. While research on digital literacies and contemporary education reforms highlights the learning potential of digital play—in particular, its value for developing skills with online communication—Sheldon faculty disciplined play by disabling it in the classroom. They did not transform kids' digital play into cultural capital for achievement as faculty did at Heathcliff.

Teachers' perceptions of students' digital forms as risks informed their day-to-day instructional practices with digital technology. Faculty at Sheldon routinely created high-stakes learning activities using digital technology that made students' digital sharing an anxiety-laden experience. Mrs. Trunchbull, an eighth-grade science teacher, led her class through a lesson on states of matter. Students each had laptops at their desk, and a projector screen was on at the front of the room with a list of every student presently in class. Speaking through a Bluetooth microphone hanging from her ear, Mrs. Trunchbull projected her voice via speakers positioned around the perimeter of the class. "When a water molecule is in cold water, what does it look like?" she said. "Draw it on your laptops. Use the trackpads. Once you draw it, hit the button to send it to me." Students then lowered their heads to their computers to draw. After just under a minute, a drawing of a molecule appeared on the screen in front of the classroom with the name "Daria" in bold on the top. "Daria is IN!" exclaimed Mrs. Trunchbull. Some students "ooh'd" and "ah'd." "How'd she do that?" asked one of the students. "She did it because she's *great*," retorted Mrs. Trunchbull. She turned her back to the students and erased Daria's answer from her computer. "Now draw me a water molecule in *hot* water." Students returned to their work, and a minute passed. "No responses? You chickens." Shortly thereafter, another drawing appeared. This time the sketching was not as clear, nor was the molecule model finished, and the name "Aaron" was posted in bold at the top. "Aaron . . . ," said Mrs. Trunchbull, pausing for a moment. "I don't even know what to say?" Students all laughed, and Aaron was quiet and looked down at his computer. "Should we print this and put it on the wall so your parents can see it on open house day? Who says eighth-graders can't do art!"

In this example, Aaron's shared online creation was met with ridicule by the class. At Sheldon, education technologies were used in ways that created opportunities for high-stakes learning and public humiliation if students answered incorrectly. Moreover, the digital youth cultural activities that were valued at Heathcliff, like video games, social media, and online collaboration, were strictly restricted at Sheldon. Teachers at Sheldon maintained their own legitimacy as authorities in the face of their students, whom they saw as digitally skilled threats, by imposing sanctions for online participation that did not meet teachers' standards. This comparison between the Heathcliff and Sheldon approaches illustrates the limitations of cultural mobility theory in education. Students at both schools exhibited similar digital skills from play online. But teachers disciplined their play differently: Sheldon communicated to students that their playful pursuits online were threatening to achievement and thus denied their potential as cultural capital for learning. School socialization theory is thus a closer approximation of what we observe so far, in that teachers imagine the different labor market potential of their students and then subtly manage their creative potential in ways that guide them toward class-differentiated paths. But it's not just about class. The way teachers imagined the potential of these students was clearly shaped by assumptions about not just class but student race-ethnicity as well.

DIGITAL LITERACIES FOR LABOR AT CÉSAR CHÁVEZ MIDDLE SCHOOL

Sheldon teachers policed students' digital youth play and did not teach digital skills. I was surprised, therefore, to find that Chávez taught many of the same digital skills with technology that Heathcliff students received. However, Chávez teachers imagined their students as twenty-first-century laborers that rely on digital skills for working-class jobs. Chávez thus disciplined play by constructing students' digital play as irrelevant, even as instructors taught school-sanctioned skills with internet use, digital presentations, and programming basics.

Chávez teachers shared a perception of the later-life trajectory of their working-class, Latinx youth that seemed to inform their expectations for learning with digital technology. Teachers routinely described their students as "hardworking immigrants" from "damaged homes." Their parents were deemed to be assimilating immigrants who trusted teachers with their children's education. Ms. Duffey, a seventh-grade science teacher, argued that students' digital play was not going to help them get a working-class job:

> These kids aren't naturally gifted at technology; those skills playing video games don't translate to school. So they have fast phones? So what? The kids we teach, if we are being realistic, they need skills for hands-on jobs, like how to fix a new-wave car. If they learn technology it's for that purpose.

At Chávez, teachers constructed their lessons in ways that imparted technology skills they believed were valuable for working-class jobs. Teachers did not, however, imagine working-class jobs necessarily to be ones of material production. Ms. Gellar, a sixth-grade math teacher, elaborated:

> I don't know that these kids are going into managerial positions after school, but they need to know a different set of skills than it used to be in factories. They need basic skills in using computers, research, programming, even making websites. That's the future for these kids.

Teachers at Chávez said that they were helping their students by teaching them many new literacies, like computer use, website navigation and construction, and even programming, because they believed these skills would prepare them for a twenty-first-century factory. This imagined path of their students is firmly in line with the assertion from school socialization theory that teachers hold close sets of beliefs about the labor outcomes of their students and then socialize their students along that path. It shows how other statuses, including race-ethnicity and nativity, are critical components of this teacher imaginary. Further, teachers did not view working-class Latinx youth as academic threats, as some literature has suggested.[29] As a consequence, students were indeed taught digital skills. But as I illustrate, this construction motivated a disciplinary orientation to students' digital play that rendered their creative pursuits online irrelevant. Thus, even while these students were not seen as threats to learning as at Sheldon, Chávez faculty disciplined digital play in ways that denied its use as cultural capital for achievement.

Teachers at Chávez constructed a division between valued digital skills taught in class and what they deemed to be less useful digital play that young people brought to school. For example, Mr. Weber, an eighth-grade history teacher, agreed that his students were "digital natives" in the sense that they used technologies for fun. "They're all, especially the boys, really great at video games," he said. "But if they are going to succeed in high school and at a job, they have to be comfortable with keyboarding. They have to be able to do research and turn in papers, and they don't know how to do that. It's basic skills." In teachers' view, basic skills constituted types of technology use that were school sanctioned. They did not see video gameplay as a potentially valuable pursuit, even while acknowledging that boys, in particular, may have a leg up at video gameplay. Other faculty similarly remarked that if students were tech savvy, it was only for texting or using social media, not for academics like website navigation or research. Although the earlier analysis of students' digital play revealed that Chávez students did, in fact, develop digital skills from their play online with friends, teachers curtailed students' digital forms from becoming cultural capital for learning.

When pressed about the value of kids' digital play, teachers explained that while digital play was distinctly separate from school-valued activities for learning, it was a highly appropriate *reward* for completed work. Ms. Grey, a sixth-grade language arts teacher at the school, explained that gaming was a mostly harmless treat after all the work her students completed. "I mean, these kids are just trying so hard," she sighed. "It's not that I'm against video games, it's just that they're not going to help them reach their goals. Once they've done their work, it's how they can blow off steam and be kids." Like students at Heathcliff, Chávez students learned digital skills like website construction and programming basics. But while Heathcliff faculty positioned play as inseparable from work, Chávez teachers constructed play as a reward for work where they could finally relax and be themselves. "I mean, yeah, they can mess around in *Minecraft* and build castles or whatever and be creative," said Ms. Woodside, a seventh-grade language arts teacher at Chávez. "That's kids being themselves and they need that. If we do our jobs well as teachers, we can teach the skills they need in class and still make time for the fun stuff." At Chávez, teachers acknowledged that play is a site for kids to express their creativity, but distinctly separated students' creative expression from learning basic skills for digital labor.

Teachers' beliefs about the separation between students' digital play and school-valued "basic skills" with digital technology filtered into daily classroom instruction. I attended a multiweek series of classes about the value of education taught by Ms. Embry, a seventh-grade language arts teacher. At the end of two weeks, students were to create a series of written documents on their iPads that explained their views of the value of education using research citations from the internet. In each class, students worked independently on their iPads at their desks. Ms. Embry walked around the classroom, hands behind her back, and peered at students' screens. "I know you guys love to type like how you text, using little emoticons and spelling 'you' with the letter 'u,' " she said in one class. "That's fine for your friends, but that's not what will get you a good grade here." Rather than integrate features from students' own peer cultures, as Heathcliff faculty found ways to include kids' video gameplay and social media, teachers routinely positioned these digital forms as irrelevant to learning, instead emphasizing other skills.

As at Heathcliff and Sheldon, some students at Chávez also played *Minecraft* for fun. Consistent with other uses of technology for digital play, *Minecraft* was seen as unhelpful for learning basic skills, but appropriate as a reward for completing schoolwork. On one afternoon, students in Mr. Chase's seventh-grade science class were in a free work session to complete a lab assignment. Some students had completed their lab and were poking around on their phones. One student, in particular, appeared to be playing *Minecraft*. As Mr. Chase walked around the room to check on students and help as needed, he spotted the youth playing *Minecraft*, chuckled, and turned to the room. "You guys, I know you'd rather be preparing for the night right now," he said. Mr. Chase himself played *Minecraft* and was referring to what happens in the game when day turns to night: players must build shelters to be ready to defend themselves, because zombies come out. "I don't want to be that guy, but I need to make sure you've finished all your work before I can let you have fun. Raise your hand so I can check your work before you pull out your phones to play." As with Sheldon faculty, Chávez teachers did not find digital play to be educational. But while Sheldon teachers saw digital play as threatening to learning, Chávez faculty simply thought it was irrelevant. They positioned it as a fun reward for the laborious work that they believed would help their students to get ahead.[30] In contrast to Heathcliff, though, play like *Minecraft* was never seen as an opportunity to integrate kids' creativity with learning processes and give students some ownership over the curriculum.

I also observed Ms. Bryant, a faculty member and the school technology lab manager, teach a class on computer programming using software called Scratch. Students were permitted to work independently on their computers, using Scratch to complete challenges that teach the basics of logic to animate a cat on the screen. As part of Scratch's design, students could remix different types of audio or image files of their choice into a computer program. "You are free to use whatever media you want to complete the challenge," Ms. Bryant instructed. "But remember, at the end of the day I don't care how pretty your SpongeBob looks. You only get full points if you solve the problem." Although some assignments at Chávez provided semistructured opportunities for students to follow their own interests, like digital media from the SpongeBob television show, teachers disciplined play by treating those interests as ultimately irrelevant to schooling. If cultural mobility theory were correct, we would expect that students with similar digital skills would see their digital play treated as educationally valuable, no matter the school. However, Chávez students were taught basic digital skills but, unlike Heathcliff students, were not permitted to develop the creative potential of those skills. Rather, school socialization had the effect of social stratification through teachers' different disciplinary approaches to digital play. At Chávez, teachers' race- and class-inflected assumptions about their students' labor market potential led them to discipline their working-class Latinx students' digital play as irrelevant to school. Instead, digital play was a reward for educationally valuable digital labor reminiscent of the shop-room floor.

DISCIPLINING PLAY AT SCHOOL

Digital divides, both at home and at school, are shrinking, and so-called "digital youth" experience youth culture as digitally mediated. These generational similarities in digital skills among youth could create opportunities, particularly for minoritized groups and working-class students, to translate their digital youth cultural forms into valuable cultural capital at school. Teachers, especially at schools serving less-privileged students, are positioned to promote cultural mobility by integrating the digital play young people bring to school as a meaningful part of the learning experience. As the literature on technology and education suggests, doing so may mitigate existing inequalities.

Yet the social dynamics within these three technology-rich middle schools are better explained by theories of social reproduction. Although the student populations of each school varied by race and class, students did indeed share similar skills in online communication and digital production that they learned from play online. However, the schools had different disciplinary orientations to kids' digital play that had the effect of reproducing inequality.

I found that teachers' shared beliefs about students informed their disciplinary orientations to students' digital play. These orientations varied by school and determined whether the digital skills students brought to school were transformed into valuable cultural capital for achievement. At César Chávez Middle School, teachers saw the digital play of their working-class Latinx students as worthless compared with the more academic "basic skills" with technology they instead chose to teach. Students were told that their peer communications, experiences with video games, and interest-driven play with online images and video had no relationship to schooling. These students received lessons in digital technology but were taught to minimize their creative potential while at school.

At Sheldon Junior High, teachers' disciplinary orientation drove a conception of students' digital play as not simply irrelevant but also threatening to learning. Teachers saw signs of students' digital forms, including peer communications, video game-playing, and online production, as signals that students would use digital technologies to

SCHOOL	TEACHER ORIENTATION	INSTRUCTIONAL PRACTICE
Heathcliff Academy (Wealthy, White)	Play is essential to school	Students' digital forms translated into cultural capital for achievement
Sheldon Junior High (Middle-class, Asian)	Play is threatening to school	Students' digital forms heavily policed and regulated, denied cultural capital
Cesar Chavez Middle (Working-class, Latinx)	Play is irrelevant to school	Students' digital forms positioned as useless, denied cultural capital

TABLE 2.1: Disciplinary Orientations to Digital Play and Achievement

hack, cheat, and subvert their authority. Like those of Chávez youth, Sheldon students' digital skills were not transformed into cultural capital at school. Rather, teachers used digital technologies to construct a competitive learning environment in which achievement was measured mostly by traditional evaluations in the form of tests.

While Chávez and Sheldon teachers' disciplinary orientations to digital play inhibited its capacity to foster learning, Heathcliff teachers actively promoted an overlap between digital play and work as an agenda for learning. Teachers' assumptions about students' privileged position, combined with expectations that youth bring generation-specific digital skills, fueled instructional practices that transformed students' digital forms into valued cultural capital for achievement. Teachers actively used a metaphor of bringing students' "garages" to school to suggest that students should, as part of a learning experience, tinker and mess around with digital technology as a process for learning.

What this suggests is that the existing story of cultural inequality—that if kids possessed the same currency of valued skills, then teachers would similarly reward students with good grades—is false. In this chapter I show *how* this is so: teachers invoke different disciplinary approaches to play, and thus the digital know-how students develop through play, depending on the race and class of their student population. To refer back to the teacher-shopkeeper metaphor shared earlier, even though students may possess the same currency, the school environment determines whether that same currency is accepted or not in exchange for educational achievement. In the next chapter, I show *why* the school-storefront might perceive the value of similar cultural knowledge differently. I locate the sources of teachers' disciplinary orientations in an interaction between the racialized and classed meanings teachers bring and the workplace dynamics at their school.

3

——

WHERE DISCIPLINARY

ORIENTATIONS COME FROM

Social reproduction theorists gesture toward the labor market outcomes that teachers imagine for their students as a primary driver of teacher discipline. Specifically, this literature says that teachers think wealthy kids are headed to leadership roles and working-class kids to the factory shop floor. Teachers then subconsciously cultivate them for these paths at school.[1] I stumbled upon a curious, contradictory phenomenon as I interviewed teachers to unearth perceptions of their students: teachers would share multiple, conflicting stereotypes about their students of color in interviews, but they exhibited only one belief in the classroom and elsewhere at school.

For example, I interviewed Ms. Limon, a seventh-grade math teacher at Chávez, and asked her about her current pupils.[2] "My students are mostly Hispanic and a lot of them come from damaged homes," she explained, her eyes narrowed with genuine concern. "But these kids work so hard to try to make it in this world. Their parents really trust us with their children." Later on in the interview, as I asked about her experiences teaching at other schools, she volunteered a very different stereotype about working-class Latinx youth. "I used to work at a school in Illinois before coming to teach at Chávez," she said, shaking her head. "We had so many behavior issues there. It was mostly Hispanic kids from broken homes with lots of issues from family. I swear half of our energy was staying on top of discipline."

Just a few days after meeting with Ms. Limon, I was at Sheldon Junior High to interview Mr. McNally, an eighth-grade language arts teacher. I asked him, too, to describe his current student body. "You have to watch out for them," he told me. "These Asian kids are under so much pressure that they'll cheat or do anything to do well. It's because they're raised by Tiger Moms." Later on in the interview, I asked him to describe students he's worked with at other schools, and he told me he had worked at a school with a similar demographic. "Teaching there was like cake," he said. "They're just so damn smart, it's that Asian culture thing, you know? So well behaved. They call it model minority for a reason!"

As I asked the primarily White middle-class teachers in this study to reflect on student populations they had taught, both at their present place of work and at other schools, I learned that they all shared two competing views of their students of color: two ways of perceiving working-class Latinx students, and two constructions of middle-class Asian American students. At Chávez, teachers described their Latinx students as "benevolent immigrants," while deeming Latinx students they had worked with elsewhere as likely to be "future gang members." Faculty at Sheldon portrayed their Asian students through a lens of "cutthroat hackers," whereas Asian students they had taught elsewhere were "model minorities."

These stereotypes are not exactly new to scholarship on race and immigration. Qualitative work illustrates the diversity of teachers' assumptions about students of color. As an example, some studies find that White teachers, invoking a form of paternalism, construct working-class Latinx students as hardworking immigrants, whereas other studies show teachers stereotyping Latinx students as having criminal intents. Other research shows that teachers construct upwardly mobile Asian American students as model minorities, or bound for success as a consequence of racial affiliation, whereas some work portrays such youth as cutthroat competitors.[3]

Despite exhibiting multiple sets of stereotypes about their students of color, teachers at each school could not muster any comparable racialized imagery about their White pupils. When I asked teachers at each school to describe their White students, most seemed confused, would not describe them as "White students," and instead referred to them as "students" or used their individual names. "I don't think being White has anything to do with it," huffed Ms. Ullman, a seventh-grade teacher at Sheldon. "I treat my students individually; that's the best way to educate them, based on their individual needs." When asked about their White students, teachers at these schools said that students are too unique to really generalize about them even though they had generalized about their Asian and Latinx student populations earlier in the interview.

Where might the teachers in this study get their ideas about students of color, and why is Whiteness so invisible? Theories of colorblind racism argue that contemporary racial ideology gives Whites a set of tools to at once "not see color" and at the same time continue to exhibit very problematic racist beliefs and practices that benefit Whites at the expense of people of color.[4] One such manifestation of colorblind racism is Whites' racial stereotyping.[5] Racial stereotypes, like those shared by the largely White teachers in this study, typically place blame for the collective experiences of an entire racial-ethnic group (like poor academic performance) on students of color they encounter. Such stereotypes thus also operate as an ideological mechanism that shapes how students of color are taught—treated not as individuals, but instead as an unfair and inaccurate representation of academic worth.

Some might argue that some stereotypes, like "model minority" or "benevolent immigrant," can help students by portraying them in a positive light. But even these "positive" stereotypes still embody and reproduce Whites' colorblind ideology through cultural racism. Stereotypes like that of the "model minority" do the work of collapsing the lived experience of an entire racial-ethnic population into discrete beliefs that generalize without paying mind to the individual character of a person. In the present study, these generalizations simply did not exist for White people, who were instead treated as individuals. Moreover, teachers were shocked and upset at the notion that White students could comparably be defined by a sweeping generalization about their racial-ethnic category. What this does is create an asymmetry in explaining why good or bad things happen to people: "model minorities" are smart because of their racial-ethnic group, whereas Whites' intelligence is based on their individual capabilities and effort. Stereotypes about model minorities put undue pressure on students subject to this myth. That pressure can, if not substantively upheld by such students, lead them to feel as though they are failing the image of their entire racial-ethnic group.[6] White students do not experience such expectations as a consequence of their racial-ethnic affiliation.

In summary, the literature on race and ethnicity points to the shared ideology of colorblindness among White faculty as the reason why they exhibit racial stereotypes for people of color and do so under the guise of not "seeing" race. When their students weren't around, the faculty in this study would share lengthy stories about their students of color with me and with each other that they argued were reflective of students' entire racial-ethnic groups. These beliefs, I find, drive divergent disciplinary approaches to digital play based on the race and class of their student body.

What this literature did not help me to disentangle is how these teachers made sense of the multiple stereotypes they possessed about the same racial-ethnic student populations. How is it that the same set of teachers can exhibit a stereotype of Latinx students at their present school as "benevolent immigrants" and describe Latinx students they have taught elsewhere as "criminals"? Both are certainly sets of culturally racist imagery that exist in our social landscape, but theories of race and racism do not explain how people adjudicate between *multiple* stereotypes of racial-ethnic groups with varied meanings and still produce unequal outcomes.[7]

Solving this puzzle was among the most challenging aspects of this project. I decided to directly ask teachers why they thought I was encountering these multiple, contradictory stereotypes about students of color. Most faculty exhibited the same colorblind response: they denied that such stereotypes existed despite having just shared them. But a few teachers suggested that the sources of their perceptions were more complicated than they had first thought. At the end of an interview with Ms. Gellar, a sixth-grade math teacher at Chávez, I told her that existing research would expect us to find that a school serving working-class Latinx youth would have more behavioral issues and disciplinary sanctions at school. I asked her why students at Chávez were different from those at her other school whom she had described as future criminals. She paused and said:

> The way people react here at Chávez is a lot more civilized
> than some other places I've worked where teachers not only

confront students, but also get in other teachers' faces. In my experience at different schools, how your teachers are with each other is how your kids are with each other. Last year, the vice principal referred to this school as Disneyland in terms of discipline compared to other schools with the same demographic of kids. That difference comes from how teachers at this school see these kids differently, not as behavioral problems, but as people who have a bigger story to them than what we see in one moment in class. The administrators are the same with the teachers as they are with the kids, too. The trust just flows. If you take the same group of kids and put them in other schools, they will act completely differently. It's about what you surround these kids with.

Ms. Gellar's take pointed not simply to individual teachers' beliefs but to the role of relationships among faculty and administrators in shaping perceptions of students of color. What do we know about the ways in which faculty *workplaces* affect the perceptions that teachers draw upon when disciplining students' digital play?

I find that theories of organizational culture explain when and why teachers draw on such racialized and classed stereotypes of their students. The largely White and middle-class teachers in this study brought to school varied stereotypes about their students of color. At the same time, as members of school organizations, teachers share norms and expectations of one another that govern their relationships not only with students but also with other faculty. Teachers at Chávez referred to the faculty and administrators there as "in it together"; faculty at Sheldon instead described their working environment as "every man for himself"; and teachers at Heathcliff pointed to a shared expectation of elite servitude. These workplace dynamics, which were experienced by faculty as part of their jobs, are what scholars of organizations refer to broadly as organizational culture.[8] Institutional underpinnings of what it means to work in education are inflected through the social location of each school: schools' own histories shape the taken-for-granted beliefs, routines, and rituals that school inhabitants experience.

Perhaps the most substantive analysis of how teacher workplace dynamics can shape student achievement is in work by Anthony Bryk and Barbara Schneider on what they call relational trust.[9] Using a series of survey items that estimate trust at several levels (teacher-principal, teacher-teacher, and teacher-parent), they show that elementary schools with higher overall trust levels have greater student gains in reading and math than do those with weaker trust levels. Relational trust, they argue, serves as a resource for school members to address day-to-day issues and adapt to institutional change, and encourages teachers to do more to serve their students, leading to academic gains.

But while their work shows that the presence of such trust leads to overall student gains, schools that are either racially mixed or dominated by Black or Latinx populations are significantly less likely to be associated with trust among teachers. Bryk and Schneider qualify this by suggesting that in such schools, "to interpret any misunderstanding and miscommunication along racial lines is natural," making it harder for teachers to maintain trust.[10]

By my reading, there are still a series of unanswered questions about how and why teacher workplaces may shape race and class differences in pedagogy. First, we cannot assume that differences in student racial-ethnic school composition will inherently lead to differences in trust among faculty. There may be particular historical shifts at the school and the outlying community that explain why racial divisions occur and what those divisions mean to school inhabitants. Nor can we assume, where trust among faculty exists, that students of color may experience less marginalization during instruction. While trust among faculty may indeed influence teaching, it does not eliminate racial structures, such as teachers' stereotyping students of color with respect to their academic capacity. Further, while measuring student achievement is important, it is equally important to document the underlying effect of school socialization in shaping a student's sense of creative self-worth and future aspirations. Trust among faculty could lead to student academic gains, but there may be differences in whether students believe their successes will help them climb the opportunity ladder. How do both workplace dynamics, like teacher trust, and perceptions of student demographics, such as racialized and classed stereotypes of students, shape teachers' day-do-day instructional practices?

With the data from this study, I can't pinpoint where teachers obtained racialized and classed stereotypes of their students, but I can show whether or not teachers possessed those stereotypes and how they deployed them at school. What I ultimately argue is that this process of faculty stereotype selection is how colorblind racist ideology is filtered through the school organizational environment. In this study, I found that in the context of an interview, teachers displayed awareness of multiple constructions of Asian American youth as either model minorities or Tiger Mom-raised, cutthroat hackers. But only teachers at Heathcliff saw their Asian American students as the former and only teachers at Sheldon saw them as the latter. Teachers at Heathcliff shared an orientation of serving elites (their students) as a consequence of parental pressures, and this workplace dynamic "fits" with the model minority imagery they described during interviews. At Sheldon, however, teachers shared a threat orientation to their students as a consequence of how faculty interpreted neighborhood demographic shifts as a violation of their racial and social boundaries. This view of students as threats aligned with the cutthroat hacker imagery they described during interviews.

Faculty also reported a similar set of beliefs about Latinx students as either benevolent immigrants or future criminals, but only teachers at Chávez saw their Latinx students as the former and only teachers at Sheldon saw them as the latter. Teachers at Chávez shared a caretaker orientation to their students as an extension of the familial, "in it together" mentality that carried over from their transition from an elementary school to a middle school. This caretaker orientation aligned with the benevolent immigrant imagery that teachers described during interviews. At Sheldon, however, the aforementioned threat orientation also applied to their Latinx students, and faculty at that school thus drew upon stereotypes of children as criminals.

Faculty workplace norms and teachers' perceptions of students of color are directly related and drive their approach to kids' digital play. Sheldon faculty described their workplace as "every man for himself," rife with hostility, teacher-to-teacher surveillance, and competition.

This toxic dynamic among Sheldon faculty drove perceptions of middle-class Asian American youth as "cutthroat hackers" and Latinx students as "future gang members." Teachers at Sheldon therefore saw kids' digital play as inherently threatening to schooling, and they disciplined play for the youth of color by denying its potential as cultural capital for achievement. Chávez faculty reported their workplace as "in it together," a family-like dynamic of support and collaboration. The "in it together" dynamic among Chávez faculty drove perceptions of working-class Latinx youth as "hardworking immigrants"; teachers thus saw kids' digital play as not threatening, but irrelevant. Teachers instead focused school-sanctioned activities on rote digital labor that they believed would help their students get jobs someday as contemporary worker bees.

An interesting consequence of Whiteness is how its invisibility privileged White students no matter the school context. Literature in this space argues that Whiteness is typically seen not as a racial identity or categorization but rather as "normal" and muted, whereas other people of color are systematically marked. Whiteness's invisibility is cited as a critical component serving the reproduction of racial structure in that it imposes a power asymmetry through day-to-day perception: the actions of Whites are seen as individual, whereas those of people of color are interpreted as a representation of their racial-ethnic group.[11] This played out exactly in Sheldon and Heathcliff, the two schools with White students, but in a paradoxical way. White students' successes at Heathcliff were seen as a result of their individual achievement, whereas Asian students' successes were seen as a result of being Asian ("model minority"). Asian and Latinx students' bad behavior at Sheldon was seen as a result of being Asian (Tiger Mom-raised hacker) or Latinx (felonious), whereas White students were ignored or punished less severely. Whiteness' invisibility both elevated White students and shielded them from potential sanctions that students of color experienced.

In tracing how teachers' stereotypes were variably employed at school and in the classroom, I show how their workplace culture created a calculus by which one stereotype was selected for work at each school. I build on our understanding of mechanisms of social reproduction by linking the racialized and classed content of teachers' perceptions of their students and the faculty workplace culture, a two-piece formula that shapes how teachers discipline play differently based on the race and class of their student body.

TEACHERS' PERCEPTIONS

Faculty at César Chávez Middle School saw their predominately working-class Latinx students as benevolent, hardworking immigrants. Mr. Weber, an eighth-grade history teacher, said, "At Chávez, it's basically Latinx or Hispanic students, and I would say lower middle class or working class. Really high proportion of single-parent families or where the father is in jail or they don't even know the father. But they come to this school looking for a better life for their kids." Ms. Embry, an seventh-grade language arts teacher, noted that "a lot of kids here have uneducated parents from Mexico that only speak Spanish, and they want to be supportive of their kid in school but just don't know how." As in much of the literature on perceptions of Latinx students in public schools, these White middle-class teachers at Chávez constructed their students in classed and racialized ways, but their depictions were of assimilating immigrants attending school to reach for the American Dream.

Teachers at Sheldon Junior High also described their students through the lens of race and class and did so with imagery of smart yet cutthroat Asian immigrant youth. Ms. McDonough, a seventh-grade language arts teacher, explained:

> The typical student here is pretty high achieving. Mostly Asian and very good at taking tests, but not very good independent thinkers. I think they have a lot of fear of doing something wrong because they're raised by these Tiger Moms who will not let them out of the house unless they do well. We have some very gifted kids who are already taking the SATs and scoring high, but they lack some of the humanity kids this age should have because of how they're raised.

Like Ms. McDonough, Mr. McNally expressed frustration that his eighth-grade students were raised to be so test-focused. "They're only as good as how they are on a test," he said. "In Asian culture, their livelihoods are about tests. The benchmark in China is about tests. We're creating people who can't think or can't problem solve, but they're good at tests." Teachers also relayed that their students' cut-throat orientation extended into major disciplinary issues. "We've had a bunch of suspensions this year because these Asian kids are so good at using technology that they hack our online system," said Ms. Finnerty, an eighth-grade science teacher. "One student broke into a teacher's website and locked her out. They'll do anything to do well." At Sheldon Junior High, teachers drew on racialized imagery of Asian American students as test-focused, Tiger Mom-raised youth who are intelligent but also potential threats.

Sheldon served a more diverse student body than the other two schools in this study, and when I asked faculty to reflect on their Latinx student population, they drew on stereotypes of students who are Latinx as threats, diverging from how Chávez faculty positioned Latinx students as immigrant achievers. Ms. Leary, a sixth-grade language arts teacher at Sheldon, described her Latinx students as "unruly": "They don't do as well academically as the Asian students here," she said, "and so they start a lot of fights with them. I'm sure they learn it from their culture at home." Mr. Oruche, a sixth-grade language arts teacher, similarly described his Latinx students as troublemakers. "Those students, especially the boys, are much more aggressive than the other students," he said. "Our Asian students may be crazy competitive, but they won't resort to fists like the Latinx kids here do." Whereas Chávez faculty saw their Latinx students as hardworking immigrants, Sheldon faculty saw both Asian American and Latinx students through a "threat" orientation: as cutthroat hackers and violence-prone troublemakers, respectively.

Meanwhile, at Heathcliff, teachers did not have much to say about their majority White student body beyond typical banter that they were "good kids," "very smart," and "come from good families." Faculty at Sheldon described their smaller population of White students similarly. Whiteness was not a readily accessible status to teachers, which resonates with research that positions Whiteness as invisible. However, Heathcliff did have a small Asian American population, and teachers shared race-based assumptions about these youth. "Well, you know what they say," said Mr. Blendell, an eighth-grade math teacher. "Asian kids really do fit that model minority stereotype. Our other students could learn a lot from them." Another teacher, Mr. Gates, described Asian students in his music classes. "They're so gifted at music," he said. "I think I read somewhere that Asian culture celebrates music. It's such a beautiful thing." Heathcliff faculty described their Asian American students with a benign achiever orientation, a stark contrast to the threat lens applied to Asian American students at Sheldon.

Despite their ability to narrate lengthy race- and class-tinged stories about the students at their current school, teachers described students of similar demographics at other schools where they had worked in starkly contrasting ways. In other words, teachers recalled different racial stereotypes depending on the school where they taught. Among Sheldon teachers who had worked with Asian populations elsewhere, these constructions were more consistent with those shared by Heathcliff faculty. Ms. Nisbett, a seventh-grade science teacher at Sheldon, said that she had worked at another school in the area that served mostly Asian American children. "My job there was so easy; the kids were just so darn smart," she said. "Quiet, but smart. I think it's part of Asian culture, they're just on such good behavior all the time." Ms. McDonough, a seventh-grade language arts teacher who worked previously at a school three hours away from Sheldon, explained that her other school "had a mixture of White, Asian, and Latinx students, but the brightest were the Asian students. I just don't know what it is. They always know the answer to the questions. It's no wonder they end up at great schools like UCLA or Cal [Berkeley]." Recounting his teaching at a school in a different part of the state, Mr. Kenworth, an art teacher at Sheldon, said that his old school also had a high Asian population. "They did well in class because of the cultural thing," he explained. "Their parents are first-generation and grew up in a different country, and came here for opportunity and the educational system. They just want their kids to do better for themselves. They were good kids." Teachers at Sheldon described Asian students at their current school as racialized threats, but when referring to Asian students at other schools where they had worked, they drew on nonthreatening, model minority imagery. I discuss later how school culture plays a powerful role in shaping the use of these stereotypes. But these two sets of beliefs likely reflected the range of teachers' beliefs about Asian American youth.

In a similar flip, teachers at Chávez described Latinx students at other schools as very different from Latinx youth at their current school. For example, Ms. Woodside, a seventh-grade language arts teacher at Chávez, also had worked at another school with mostly poor Latinx youth. "It was one of those inner-city schools; lots of kids who are in Latinx gangs or who have siblings who are in them," she said. "Teaching at a place like that was like teaching future gang members." Another teacher, Ms. Gellar, did her student teaching at an inner-city school, as well. "A lot of the kids there were latchkey kids whose parents came here from Mexico, or one parent is even still back there," she explained. "These kids were in gangs, had probation officers, absolutely no support at home. Behavioral issues were out of control." While teachers described students at Chávez with a kind of "new immigrant" narrative, these same teachers who had worked at other schools with similar student demographics instead characterized those youth as future criminals. These teachers' dual perceptions of students with similar race and class statuses likely represented the repertoire of stereotypes available to construct Latinx youth.

I also probed extensively to try to unearth any associations teachers had for their White students, but could not find any imagery or stereotypes comparable to those that were so immediately available to teachers when describing their Latinx or Asian students. When I asked teachers at each school to describe either their few White students or White students they had taught elsewhere, most seemed confused, would not refer to them as "White students" to mobilize their responses as they did for Asian or Latinx students, but instead referred to them as "students" or by individual student's names.

"I don't think being White has anything to do with it," said Ms. Ullman, a seventh-grade teacher at Sheldon. "I treat my students individually; that's the best way to educate them: based on their individual needs." When asked about their White students, teachers at these schools said that students are too unique to generalize about, even though they had generalized about their Asian and Latinx student populations earlier in the interview. These findings align well with the findings of scholarship on the social construction of Whiteness that it operates invisibly. Nonwhites are marked by racial categories and are thus *other* to the normative category of White identity. Although scholars have written on the role of White invisibility in creating and reproducing White privilege and power, I find that it additionally protects White students from being seen according to sweeping racial-ethnic stereotypes at schools where students of color are the majority. Rather than being portrayed by teachers through one of multiple stereotypes about their racial-ethnic group, like Asian and Latinx students, White students are instead seen as individuals whose successes and failures are their own.

The few teachers of color in this study sometimes shared conflicting stereotypes about their students of color similar to those presented by White teachers. Others tried to avoid discussion with me about the topic during interviews. To be frank, I did not expect that faculty of color would be immediately comfortable talking with me (a White male) about racial stereotypes in their student body. One interview I conducted with Mr. Hagan, a self-identified Mexican American who taught sixth-grade science at Chávez, teases out some of this tension. When I first asked him to describe the student body at Chávez, he tightened up. "Matt," he said sternly, eyebrows furrowed, "just because they're Latino doesn't mean they're bad kids." He likely had no reason not to assume I was searching for such stereotypes to legitimize the very stereotypes his White colleagues carried and expressed at school. But even if faculty of color exhibited a point of view that contested the pervasive stereotypes of students of color shared by White teachers, they remained a very small percentage of the faculty population.[12]

The predominant pattern among the largely White body of teachers at each school was to share contradictory perceptions of Asian and Latinx students, essentially revealing two sets of beliefs they use to construct students of color. I prompted them to reconcile the source of the differences. Most of the time teachers expressed difficulty putting the words together to explain why they would characterize students so differently. Some would stutter and quickly say that they meant only one of the descriptions was "right," such as when Ms. Woodside responded with a correction: "Well, there were only a *few* bad students at the other school, these kids mostly just came from tough situations." Others could not explain the source of the difference but were stern in their assertion that both characterizations were true.

Findings so far suggest that teachers' constructions of Latinx and Asian youth were indeed heterogeneous and also located in particular social environments. Whiteness, however, was invisible in each of the schools. But recall that upon being probed deeper some teachers suggested that the sources of their perceptions were more complicated than they had thought at first: they believed that faculty workplace dynamics had a hand in how they treated their students. In the next sections, I examine situational dynamics located at each of these schools. I begin each school discussion by describing the workplace dynamics that created an environment that fostered a particular set of stereotypes. I then show where these workplace dynamics came from: a consequence of schools' recent histories.

"IN IT TOGETHER" AT CÉSAR CHÁVEZ MIDDLE SCHOOL

Among teachers and staff at Chávez, the common thread was that everyone there was "in it together." This phrase represented an unofficial template for social dynamics at the school and reflected a durable set of norms for how faculty worked with one another and taught their students. During a group interview, Ms. Fillion, a sixth-grade math teacher, said, "We care about our kids and want them to do well. We have conversations about students all the time, like, 'What's up with Johnny lately?' It bonds us." Ms. Ramirez (language arts) agreed: "We are very together. We share our lessons, like, 'Here you go! I'll make copies.' Some schools, they don't do that. You're actually judged here if you aren't open about your work!"

During individual interviews with other faculty, a theme similarly surfaced over and over: the workplace dynamic at Chávez provided a shared purpose around collaboration and help and created expectations for peer support among faculty. During interviews, teachers explained to me that Chávez was "very collaborative" and described other teachers as "helpful" and "there for you" in times of need.

Ms. Roberts, a seventh-grade language arts teacher at the school, elaborated:

> The teachers at this school are *very* cohesive . . . I'll send students who need extra work or a detention to someone else; they'll send students to me because they say I have something that better supports this student. We will do that a lot. You feel like everyone is part of your family here.

The "in it together" mentality supported a normative understanding of sharing and commitment among the network of teachers at Chávez. This was especially noticeable when faculty described the experience of being a new teacher at the school. Ms. Busch, a seventh-grade science teacher, wished she had started her career at Chávez instead of elsewhere. "I mean, it's just so hard getting started as a teacher, having to learn the ropes and everything," she said. "At Chávez, we really roll out the red carpet for new teachers. We provide them with tips, mentors; share syllabi. We're all open books and are there for one another." More-established faculty reflected on the supportive culture, as well. "When I lost a parent a few years ago, it was probably one of the hardest things I've ever been through," explained Ms. Grey, a sixth-grade language arts teacher. "The teachers here pretty much descended upon me with flowers and food and so much love. They're like a family." Teachers at Chávez defined their relationship dynamic with other faculty as family-like, collaborative, and supportive.

Teachers' talk about the family-like, 'in it together' norm resonated with observed behavior during day-to-day life at the school. Faculty meetings and faculty lunchroom banter revolved around asking for or offering help with specific questions about lessons or about students they had concerns about. Over lunch, three teachers talked about one student named Jose, about whom they all shared concern. "Jose's been acting up in my [seventh-grade] class and I have no idea why. I can tell he's a smart kid but there's something up," said Ms. Woodside. "He was fine for most of my [sixth-grade] class," said Ms. Ramirez, "but toward the end of the year he was doing exactly what you were saying—something is definitely going on." Ms. Fillion waved her finger in the air and said, "That's around the same time he told me his parents are going through a divorce. We should talk to the school counselor and get this kid some help." This kind of discussion among teachers happened regularly on campus, an activity they jokingly referred to as "triage." Triage, either by helping other teachers resolve problems or by identifying students that needed other help, occupied the discussion in both formal meetings and informal settings like lunches.

Like their teachers, students at Chávez were also aware of, and embedded in, the 'in it together' way of life at the school. The youth described teachers as "like family," "strict, but really caring," and "people they can trust." Bailey (14 years old, Latinx) said that "teachers here enjoy what they're doing so it just spills over to us. We like it much more. It feels like they want us to understand. They're like mentors." Caleb (13 years old, Latinx) explained that "these teachers are super nice. They're like your Moms and Dads. They're very close to the students. They're more like family almost. That's the way they treat us and so we treat them with respect." The 'in it together' approach to teaching generated trust between teachers and students and gave students the assurance they needed to approach teachers when something was wrong. "They're more helpful here than at my other school," Mercedes (14 years old, Latinx) said. "At my other school teachers didn't even talk to us. Here if you go to them with a problem they'll actually do something. They're people you can open up to."

This family-like behavior on the part of students and teachers was represented by more than isolated incidents. The "in it together" norm summarized a meaning system associated with the network of inhabitants within this particular organization. It imposed an expectation of sharing and collaboration and encouraged people in need to speak up because they could anticipate kindness and compassion as a response. While teachers appreciated the school dynamic, meeting these expectations also occupied much of their time and energy. "It's a damn lot of work to be this nice!" said Ms. Ramirez, laughing. "But it's definitely worth it in the end, especially for the students."

At Chávez, teachers constructed their working-class Latinx students in ways consistent with their interviews—as struggling, well-intentioned immigrants—as an extension of their "in it together" mode at school. For example, I observed Mr. Weber's eighth-grade history class during first period, and he was starting a new lesson on factory labor and working conditions in the twentieth century. The formal materials for the lesson, including slides and handouts, comprised timelines that denoted phases of industrialization in the United States and selections from Upton Sinclair's *The Jungle* describing the poor conditions for workers in factories "The warmup for today," said Mr. Weber, "is your diet. What are your eating habits? Protein, carbs, et cetera . . . or McDonald's twice a week?" A student raised his hand and responded: "I'm a vegetarian!" Mr. Weber nodded. "Good for you, Frankie. You are what you eat. Anyone else?" Another student, Mary, spoke up. "My mom cooks vegetables every now and then. I eat junk food on some days. Pretty normal I think." "Thank you, Mary," said Mr. Weber. He looked to a slide on his projector and read the words aloud: "If we are such a smart nation, why do we eat crap?" He turned back to the students. "Let's investigate this. The average Mexican immigrant today makes $10/hour more in food factories than he does at any other job. The working conditions are bad, but he makes more. So why wouldn't he work there to care for his family?" Mr. Weber then turned on a clip from *Fast Food Nation* and played a scene that shows, in gripping detail, Mexican workers getting injured on the job. "Today's factory job is no different than it was in Sinclair's *The Jungle*," said the teacher. "The only difference is that the workers today are Latinos and other immigrants *just like you*." Students were silent. "This is why it's so important that you let us, at school, help you do the best you can. You need to do well and stay in school no matter what so you can make a better life for yourselves."

Although Mr. Weber's curricular plan for the day was about poor working conditions in the twentieth century, he translated the material into content that best "fit" with both the stereotype of Latinx students as suffering, well-intentioned immigrants and the school-wide orientation that saw people there as "in it together." But when I approached him after his lesson, his responses were focused only on the family-like take of his class: "Aren't they just incredible? They really need us. It's days like this that make you feel good to be a teacher." Although in interviews he described Latinx youth at a school where he previously taught as "future gang members," such a construction was not readily accessible at this school, where teachers were positioned as caretakers. The family-like orientation to work that faculty had adopted rendered "appropriate" one set of beliefs, that of the well-intentioned, immigrant Latinx, while obscuring the fact that teachers also harbored another, less favorable image of Latinx students.

I have so far described how norms among faculty shaped a collaborative, family-like orientation to their work and illustrated how these norms helped teachers select the "appropriate" belief from their available range of stereotypes of Latinx students. But where did these workplace norms come from? As I spoke with faculty and staff about the history of the school, I learned that it followed a rather unusual trajectory within the broader community. The area had seen a very large influx of Latinx people over the preceding ten years, a 21.39 percent increase, to account for just over half of the community population.[13] Its smaller, White population, 43 percent, primarily resided closer to the oceanfront, and Latinx families lived further inland. Faculty described the public school serving the White families near the ocean as a sort of paradise, and they colloquially referred to the school as "life at the beach." Houses near that oceanfront school cost, on average, $400,000, a price tag that the Latinx population, many of whom lived at the poverty level, could not afford. Chávez's neighborhood fit an increasingly common portrait of segregation in California, where Whites and people who are Latinx immigrants seemingly live in two very separate economic and social worlds despite being five miles from one another.

When asked for reasons why Chávez exhibited a family-like atmosphere that other schools serving similar student populations lacked, teachers attributed the difference to the circumstances of the school's founding. Ms. Fillion, a sixth-grade math teacher at the school, explained:

> We used to be an elementary school just under ten years ago. The district was getting too big and couldn't accommodate the many, many immigrant families that moved here. So they talked to Mr. Erickson, who was the principal of the elementary school where he and many of us worked, and convinced

him to be the head of this middle school. A bunch of us left that school to join him. Sure, the kids we teach are older, but it feels the same. We never had to leave our family.

Just under half of the faculty at Chávez migrated with Mr. Erickson from an elementary school in the district to establish this middle school. When asked about the collaborative, "in it together" workplace, they said it arose from the supportive dynamic that was expected back in the day when it was an elementary school.

Was this rosy interpretation of Chávez's origins as a collaborative workplace shared by everyone? Although faculty said they abided by the shared norms to collaborate and support one another, there were other perspectives on how it came to be. "It was like they all stormed in, smiling, on 'Team Erickson,'" said Ms. Duffey, rolling her eyes. "Don't get me wrong, Derek [the principal] is great. But these teachers that joined the school with him were already friends and give off this 'their way or the highway' kinda thing." Ms. Duffey was a science teacher at the middle school before it was reorganized and taken under the wing of Principal Erickson and his fleet of former elementary school teachers. She described the new teachers as a "clique" that carried a lot of favor with the administration. "Every time there's a new initiative or curricular push, it does feel like if you don't do it you'll be shamed if you aren't fully on board," explained Ms. Underwood, an eighth-grade math teacher who was also not part of the elementary school faculty group. "They make you feel like you're doing some moral disservice to the kids, but really they're just trying to make themselves look good." Although some faculty were put off by the clique of former elementary school faculty, they all said that they ultimately still complied with expectations of collaboration and support. "I mean, what am I going to do, not be helpful?" explained Ms. Duffey. "You'd still end up looking like the asshole who didn't help with someone's syllabus."

Despite all of this, Mr. Chase, a seventh-grade science teacher at the school, reflected that Chávez was different from other middle schools he had taught at. "At most junior high schools, the teachers have to act like the police almost, be very attentive to discipline," he explained. "But a lot of teachers here used to work with little kids. You wouldn't expect former elementary school teachers to act like cops, and we're probably better off that way." This family-like approach filtered into their school's approach to technology use at school. "We know these kids have good intentions, and so that's why we don't go crazy blocking things online or hunting their logs down on our network," said Ms. Bryant, the school's technology lab manager. "We focus on teaching them the skills we need, not punishing them for making mistakes." The history of Chávez's founding shaped the "in it together" workplace dynamic among faculty. This dynamic led teachers to think of their students as well-intentioned and made "sensible" a construction of their students as benevolent immigrants rather than the future criminals faculty described elsewhere.

"EVERY MAN FOR HIMSELF" AT SHELDON JUNIOR HIGH

Contrasting with the familial organizational dynamic at Chávez, the idea of coworkers as a family was often the butt of jokes at Sheldon. "There's this pressure to tell everyone here that 'we're a family,'" said Ms. Steele, a seventh-grade math teacher. "But my opinion is that if you're a family, you don't have to advertise it." Ms. Umberger, a seventh-grade social studies teacher, said, "Teachers here are a lot like the women in that movie *Mean Girls*. They won't let you sit with them at lunch. You're really on your own a lot of the time; it feels like it's every man for himself."

When asked to describe their relationships with coworkers at school, teachers would say over and over that they felt like it was "every man for himself." Teachers described their relationships with other teachers as "professional," and their work as very "nine-to-five," but they did not attempt to get any closer with anyone else. Mr. Penna, a physical education teacher, said that it was "not exactly buddy-buddy here. I have a life at home. I go to work to make money, that's about it." Teachers at Sheldon were guarded about themselves and their work. "I try to keep to myself except for the few teachers I'm close with," said Ms. Leary, a sixth-grade language arts teacher. "If you open up too much they'll take advantage of you or call you out with other teachers." Echoing Ms. Leary, Mr. McNally explained that if teachers decided to voice their opinions, they had to do so with caution. He recounted one time when he disagreed with another teacher during a department meeting:

> I told [the other teacher] that what she was saying was not what we had decided at an earlier meeting. She did not like that I even questioned her and she took a box of pens in front of her and threw them at another table. Treating me like I was a student! At the end of the meeting we all walked out and not one person said to her that her behavior was inappropriate. In some ways teachers are bullying each other. They tolerate everyone's unprofessionalism.

At Sheldon, the "every man for himself" sentiment summarizes the social dynamic that teachers had to wrestle with when interacting with their colleagues. Teachers were afraid to open up too much with other teachers, including sharing their opinions, for fear of being attacked.

Day-to-day life at Sheldon closely aligned with the workplace norms teachers articulated. Faculty lounge and lunch banter almost always included negative, cutting gossip about other teachers.[14] Racist and homophobic epithets were not uncommonly used in reference to other colleagues. During faculty meetings, the typical dynamic was—in the words of one teacher—"antagonistic." The principal started every meeting with an activity called "snaps," where teachers anonymously submitted words of appreciation for another teacher, which were then read in front of everyone at the meeting. Although the premise seemed harmless, teachers used these snaps as opportunities to make fun of other teachers. "Thanks to our school psychologist, who is always there for our students," the principal read from one note. Another teacher in the room snorted and said, "She's always there . . . except when she's not. She's not even here!" The room laughed. Students, too, were subject to the same types of messages from faculty and staff. Reading another "snap," the principal congratulated a teacher on running the school's first spelling bee:

> PRINCIPAL: Thank you to Nick for bringing this event
> to Sheldon!

NICK: Our new champion is Dane!

TEACHER: Now what happens to Dane?

NICK: He goes to other schools to compete.

PRINCIPAL: I want you guys to say 'Ooooooooooh!'
[waves his hands in the air]

ALL: Ooooooooooh!

PRINCIPAL: What do you think the odds are of him
going to the next level?

NICK: . . . let's just say he'll like the medallion
he won from us.

ALL: [Laughter]

PRINCIPAL: To the medallion, everybody!

In public settings at school, banter among teachers was a jagged form of joking that teachers described privately to me as "frustrating" and "tiring." "You have to always feel *on*," explained Ms. Finnerty. The "every man for himself" workplace dynamic cultivated relationships among teachers that were hostile in nature.

Teachers also put students into combative situations that were similar to those that I observed among faculty. Students almost always described their teachers as "strict" or "very tough." Daniel (15 years old, Asian), told me, "There's a handful of teachers, I don't ever want to be in their class. Many of them are mean. I have had some of them, so I know, or I hear from other students. They can be really, really strict and really, really mean, almost for no reason." In addition to the teachers being strict, students complained that classroom activities were often high-stakes. "A lot of the teachers here like to call on you at the one moment when you look distracted," said Sarah (15 years old, Asian). "If you answer correctly, you get major points from the teachers, but if you are wrong they make fun of you in front of everyone and it stinks."

On an early spring afternoon, I sat down in the back of Ms. Finnerty's eighth-grade science class. The day's lesson was a continuation of earlier work on fractions. Ms. Finnerty stood at the front of the classroom with her hands on her hips and addressed her students. "Any remaining questions before our big test next week?" One student raised his hand and asked if mixed fractions would be on the exam. "You won't have to know that for the test. If I give you a test you can rest assured knowing that it is fair." Ms. Finnerty paused for a moment, raised her eyebrow a bit, and then began pacing back and forth at the front of the room. "How many of you have ever looked at another student's test and freaked out because you were wrong?" The class was silent. "We've all done it!" she exclaimed. "Cheat and didn't mean to. Just *tell* me you did it and I'll give you a new question." Ms. Finnerty then abruptly pointed at a boy in the middle of the room. "Bobby!" He jumped a bit in his chair. "So how do you do well on the test?" Bobby looked down at his desk and squirmed in his seat. Growing impatient, Ms. Finnerty raised her hands in the air. "You dumb dumbs! If you're smart and keep good notes, you'll get into the honors placement for next year. And tests don't mean next to nothin'! Let's pretend your parents are from a 'traditional culture.'" She used her fingers to make air quotes. "Your parents can lock you in your room and shove math down your throat, but can they *apply* geometry?" Ms. Finnerty put her right hand on her chest, and raised the other. "Say *I am smart!*" Students replied, "*I am smart!*"

Immediately following the lesson, I approached Ms. Finnerty to ask if I could run a few questions by her about that day's class. "Matt, I'll tell you I barely ever remember what I'm doing when I'm up there," she told me. When I approached other teachers with specific questions after their lessons, they also often said that they were "on autopilot" and could barely remember anything beyond their original lesson plan. "You gotta be tough with these kids," Ms. Finnerty explained. "If you leave the door cracked open even just a little bit, they'll take advantage of you and weasel their way into getting an A." In a separate interview earlier in the year, Ms. Finnerty described Asian students at other schools as unthreatening model minorities, and so I asked why these students today did not fit that image. She paused and looked at me quizzically. "Not here," she said. "Teachers here have to watch out for themselves."

Like Ms. Finnerty, other teachers at Sheldon employed the same imagery in class as they used during interviews to describe their middle-class Asian American student population: driven, cutthroat, threatening hackers raised by "Tiger Moms." When asked about these moments, they rarely recalled these parts of the lesson. Instead, they focused on the features of teaching that demanded most of their mental energy: the "every man for himself" school norm and how it informed their relations, not only with teachers, but also with students. Teachers' beliefs about students of color and the situated workplace norms were linked together in ways that shaped instruction.

While Asian and Latinx students bore the brunt of teachers' negative stereotypes and negativity from their hostile workplace, White students evaded the effects of such dynamics. None of the White students I interviewed described examples of being called out like the ones students of color reported. Further, whenever I observed a White student exhibiting the same "punishable" behavior as an Asian or Latinx student, only the student of color was publicly chastised.[15] Over the course of the academic year, I documented thirty-seven examples from Sheldon classes where both White and either Asian or Latinx students were using a cell phone at their desks and teachers took some form of action against such use (verbal warnings, phone taken away, and/or sent to principal's office). Of those examples, none of the punished students were White students. What this suggests is that Whiteness, as an unmarked racial category, likely protected White youth from the teacher hostility directed at youth of color. The "every man for himself" faculty dynamic interacted with negative stereotypes of students of color in such a way that teachers' punitive gaze was focused on students who were racially marked. White students were comparatively unscathed.

I have thus far described how the "every man for himself" workplace norms shaped faculty members' interactions with one another and with their students. This dynamic led teachers to view Asian American and Latinx youth as threats rather than as model minorities or benevolent immigrants. Interestingly, the invisibility of Whiteness shielded Sheldon's White student body from the brunt of school disciplinary actions because faculty primarily drew on racial status to negotiate their perceptions of threat. But where did these workplace norms informed by particular stereotypes come from?

My fieldwork proved to be quite useful in uncovering the source of the "every man for himself" workplace environment at Sheldon. Many of the younger teachers and staff expressed their frustration with the culture among teachers, but more senior faculty articulated how this uncaring, "9 to 5" workplace had shifted over the past decade. "We all used to be so committed to our work," said Mr. Madison, an eighth-grade science teacher who had worked at the school for twenty-eight years. "But our students completely changed. This used to be a neighborhood with almost entirely middle-class White kids. All of a sudden, Asians came in and replaced everyone. It's never been the same since." Mr. Madison and other faculty were correct in noting the dramatic shift in neighborhood demographics. Over the previous ten years the Asian American population had spiked to account for 52.47 percent of the area, an increase of 20.44 percent. Whites, who had made up 40.80 percent of the neighborhood in 2000, now were only 33.19 percent, a decrease of 19.29 percent.

Senior faculty at Sheldon described this demographic shift as a threat to the happy life that they remembered as teachers. "We used to have a lot in common with these kids," said Ms. Ullman, a seventh-grade history teacher who had worked at the school for thirty-one years. "We knew where they were coming from and we knew how to support them. Today, the parents are incredibly demanding and half of them can't even speak to us in English. It's exhausting." Teachers referred to the neighborhood changes as a breach of the racial and social boundaries with which they had grown comfortable.[16]

But was it entirely racial and social differences between White teachers and students of color that fueled the "every man for himself" workplace at Sheldon? Recall that Chávez, a school that had also experienced recent demographic shifts, exhibited an entirely different and more family-like social environment. The predominately White faculty at Chávez saw themselves as caretakers of their Latinx student population. I developed a better understanding of this question by seeking out examples of how Sheldon faculty periodically tried to work against the hostile status quo at school. What I found was that other teachers—not students—circumvented these initiatives, either through the types of peer-shaming described earlier or by condemning these practices as "opening the door" to student manipulation. For example, Mr. Weeks, a seventh-grade social studies teacher, described how his workplace shaped how he approached technology use at the school. "I'm pretty good at technology, but I limit what I share with faculty and students online because I know what will happen," he said. "The kids will take advantage of you and the faculty will call you out for either trying too hard or for making them look bad." While faculty did mention students as barriers to trying to discipline students' play in a more benevolent fashion, they also blamed their coworkers for obstructing these efforts. "I think people just kind of gave up," said Ms. Brady, an eighth-grade language arts teacher who had worked at the school for fifteen years. "Nobody wanted to commit the hours that were needed to really support students. And so anybody new who really *tried* would get a lot of crap for not following the old guard." This suggests that blaming the entire student population for a hostile workplace is likely a misdirection from something rooted more deeply among faculty.

As I learned, the starkest difference between Chávez and Sheldon was that Sheldon teachers saw their students of color through a lens of upward class mobility. Chávez teachers did not report any pressure to hit particular collective marks of achievement because their students were expected to obtain, at best, working-class jobs. At Sheldon, teachers' assumptions about their middle-class Asian student population were tied to student success as an imperative. "To be quite honest with you, these Asian kids are so smart that when they don't do so well in school, the message from other teachers and administrators is that we are doing something wrong in our teaching," explained Mr. Oruche, a sixth-grade language arts teacher. Mr. Madison, who had been there when neighborhoods began to shift demographically, added that these expectations felt unfair. "I mean, what, we've been here for years, and Asian families swoop in and the expectation is that we serve them? They're all going to end up at MIT anyways." At Sheldon, faculty perceptions of the racial and class differences between teachers and students rested on an assumption that teachers were, if anything, a barrier to achievement for upwardly mobile students who were expected to do well.

Teachers maintained their own legitimacy in the face of a hostile faculty workplace by blaming race- and class-tinged student cultural differences. "I think it's easy to blame external issues, like kids or their families, rather than focus on what you deal with every day," said Ms. Moss, the school's guidance counselor. "I mean, I see what teachers are like with each other here. It's easier to bond around blaming kids than it is to have a tough conversation about how adults treat one another." In a separate interview, Ms. Bartow, the school's music teacher, shared a similar sentiment. "You see teachers putting down other students all the time—in a weird way it makes them look good. But pick a fight with another teacher? Never." Any teachers who tried to locate the source of blame in teacher culture experienced collective retaliation from other teachers.[17] By blaming students instead, teachers had a shared language around the problem that did not trigger further hostility from other faculty.

SERVING ELITES AT HEATHCLIFF ACADEMY

Parents ruled the land at Heathcliff Academy. Every faculty member and administrator at Heathcliff described the various academic standards that they imposed during instruction, but they all agreed that it ultimately came down to impressing parents. "Most of them are pretty affluent," said Mr. Filippo, a seventh-grade social studies teacher. "They are all very successful and expect their kids to succeed, too. When we teach these kids in class, we're always thinking in the back of our minds what their parents might say." This mentality of serving elites shaped Heathcliff's workplace culture. In the words of Ms. Lawson, a sixth-grade history teacher, "The feeling is if these kids don't end up getting into the best high school or college after here, it's pretty much our fault." This workplace dynamic oriented teachers to think of themselves as attendants to their gifted students.

When explaining parental pressures, Heathcliff administrators and faculty emphasized the need to assure parents of the elite treatment of students. The school even had an administrative wing that included admissions and marketing that in many ways supported this effort to communicate with parents. Ms. Abrams, an administrator for such initiatives, described the work they did to promote school achievements:

> We have a marketing strategy that is to both get interest from prospective students and cater to the needs of current students' families. We produce high-quality videos for our web-

site, and we do other videos and photos of the day-to-day at school that we push out on our social media accounts. We actively look for things to capture: school events, class projects, extracurriculars, showcasing our technology. All of this makes families feel like they made the right choice sending their kids here and encourages other families to consider applying.

Although I noticed Ms. Abrams and her teacher colleagues periodically snapping photos with their phones at school, it was not uncommon to see a more official-looking video camera set up to record events around campus. The school website and social media pages always had images or videos of school life updated with regularity. When asked about this type of promotion to parents, nearly every teacher was initially positive. "I mean, it's so important to the families here," said Ms. Lawson, a sixth-grade history teacher at the school. "What parent doesn't want to see what their children are surrounded with? Especially for what they pay just for their kids to go here." I learned that most teachers were of mixed mind about the pressure of promoting the school. "If I were being perfectly honest, it's another layer of stress," said Ms. Wu, a seventh-grade math teacher. "It's one thing to share what we're doing with parents, but it's another to feel like if you don't have something worth sharing, you're not worthwhile as a teacher. I feel like I have to adapt my curriculum in a way that makes us look good to parents." In reflecting on this type of parent communication, Heathcliff faculty felt that it was expected of them to structure their teaching with attention to parental appeasement.

Heathcliff faculty experienced a pressure similar to that facing Sheldon teachers: if students didn't succeed, the blame fell on the teachers' shoulders. The difference at Heathcliff was that faculty shared the view that they had to treat students as elites in order to "sell" their work to parents and to keep their jobs and the school afloat. This compelled faculty to put pressure on one another to appease parents. For example, I sat in on a faculty meeting where teachers and administrators discussed available budgets for their instruction. Mr. Banks, an administrator, led the meeting:

MR. BANKS: As you all know, the spring gala is a major part of the budget that we get to pay for school supplies and other events here. Remember that we had a smaller budget last year because of poorer parent turnout. We're working with the principal and marketing to do a better job, but we still need some ideas.

MS. KAUFMAN: I think we need to do a better job sharing with parents all the amazing things our students are doing. I mean, look at Dylan's yearbook online, or even some of the videos my students make for their assignments.

MS. RICHARDS: Great idea—and we need to do more of that, turn the great work our students do into activities that can be shared.

During the faculty meeting, teachers emphasized the need not only to teach students but also to make their students' achievements highly visible. This effort was driven by a desire to highlight the pedagogical process, but also by economic need. Faculty communicated similar messages to one another in less formal settings, as well. "Those kids come to me straight after his class and are half asleep," said Ms. Daniels to Mr. Gates over lunch, referring to another teacher at the school. "Students tell me they don't learn anything from him, and then I'm the one who has to spend the first thirty minutes of my time trying to wake them up." Mr. Gates shook his head, concerned. "That's not helping those kids, that's not how we do things here." At Heathcliff, faculty shared an understanding that students came first, that their students deserved an elite education, and that students' talents needed to be showcased publicly.

Parents also made their presence known on campus. In some ways, that magnified the pressure teachers faced to lavish elite treatment upon students. "It's a bit of an . . . open door policy," said Ms. Kramer, an eighth-grade science teacher. "Let's just say parents like to bake cookies a lot." Ms. Kramer was referring to what she knew I had witnessed in her classroom. Parents showed up, unannounced, with food like cookies for their students. In her class, as well as many others, parents would quite literally open the door of a class in session and set up some food in the back of the room for when class ended. "It's very much a 'help yourself' kind of thing the parents have here," said Mr. Toy, a sixth-grade math teacher. "They help themselves to your class, to your students, and there's not much we can say about it." Teachers also felt that this was another way for parents to monitor teachers. "You bet they're not here just to give me a muffin," laughed Ms. Richards, an eighth-grade science teacher. "They're here to watch us, to grade us, and gossip about us with other parents." Although I did not directly interview many parents, they would easily be confused for employees of Heathcliff simply by virtue of how regularly they were on campus. Every time I visited, I spent time in the faculty lounge. Without fail, there were parents in the lounge, either setting up preparations—food, party supplies—for an event or simply having lunch and catching up with other parents.

The parent-driven faculty workplace dynamic of elite servitude filtered into everyday teaching practices in the classroom. Ms. Abrams, a member of Heathcliff's marketing staff, explained that parents expected teachers to use the most up-to-date technologies and related methods for teaching. "We make sure that technology is a core part of our learning goals, and our parents are adamant that they [teachers] use it, too," she said. "There are only a few teachers who are against using technology in their classes, and they really stand out . . . and not for good reasons." As I spoke with faculty about technology use in class, they described keeping up-to-date with the latest tech as being in the "best interests" of their students. They also portrayed the Luddites among faculty as doing wrong by the children. "I'm no whiz at technology," said Ms. Richards, an eighth-grade science teacher, "but I do everything I can to try to keep up. The teachers who don't keep up stand out here—they just can't do the math," she said with a wink.

Ms. Richards was referring to the well-known fact that Mr. Blendell, an eighth-grade math teacher at the school, was vehemently opposed to using technology in class. "I use as little of the stuff as I can get away with," Mr. Blendell said to me. "Technology is preventing these kids from actually learning the subject material. They'll Google an equation before figuring out how to solve the problem first." But he also explained that there was a cost to standing by his principles about digital technology. "The moment a parent finds out you aren't using the latest fad, they call the principal and email other teachers and say you are doing a disservice to their kid," he said. "Parents can turn other people against you."

The faculty norm of elite servitude was vividly apparent during day-to-day life on Heathcliff's campus. Mr. MacAllister, the school's principal, encouraged me to observe Ms. Pryce's eighth-grade language arts classes, noting that she represented the "ethos" of the school. I sat in the back of the room during a class she was teaching on grammar and vocabulary. Students had their iPads on their desk and open to a related assignment they had worked on the night before. They were discussing a fill-in-the-blank sentence: "His principles were _____." "So, my dear students," said Ms. Pryce, with bravado. "The question is: are his principles incredulous, chivalrous, or altruistic?" Students mumbled among themselves, debating the possibilities. "Do I have any *scholars* with the correct answer?" she asked. Ms. Pryce regularly used words like "scholar" or "bright young minds" when referring to students as she taught them. Other teachers at the school used similar words tailored to their classes, i.e., "historians" for history, or "young scientists" in science class. A group of four students in Ms. Pryce's class narrowed their answer down to chivalrous and altruistic. "Great work! One of those two is the correct answer," said Ms. Pryce. "Adam, pick a scholar of your choice to help us figure out which one it is." Ms. Pryce and other faculty at Heathcliff positioned their students as elites and bright minds during instruction. They allowed students to interrupt their lectures with tangents and found ways to integrate those tangents into critical discussions of the material. The shared expectation of elite servitude among teachers filtered into the classroom as faculty actively framed their students as peers and soon-to-be experts in their subjects.

While students at Chávez saw teachers as parent-like and students at Sheldon saw teachers as tough disciplinarians, Heathcliff students described their teachers as being "like friends" who steered them toward success. "Teachers here are a mix of high expectations and, like, your best friends," explained Maggie (13 years old, White). "They make sure we do well but also really listen to us." Robin (13 years old, White), who also saw teachers as peers, added that "there's no strict 'you can't be friends with this teacher' rule like at other schools." Students' perception of teachers at Heathcliff was devoid of the parental or disciplinarian connotations that students at Chávez and Sheldon perceived. Instead, students emphasized that teachers were their peers who pushed them to achieve. "Every teacher here is connected to the students," explained Warren (White, 13 years old). "They may have high standards, but they're our friends, too." Heathcliff students' perception of teachers as peers that helped them succeed was a likely consequence of teachers' workplace expectation to treat students as such.

Race operated invisibly at Heathcliff for its majority-White student body, and the workplace orientation of elite servitude rendered students elite achievers in the eyes of faculty. Race was more visible to faculty, however, when it came to their small population of Asian American children. When describing Asian American students at Heathcliff, Ms. Lawson (sixth grade, history) explained that they were hardworking high achievers. "They're just so smart, and work so hard," she said. "I mean, all of our students are, of course, high-performing, but there's such a rich history in that culture to care about higher learning." Another teacher, Mr. Filippo (seventh grade, social studies), spoke similarly. "Whether it's good or bad, that 'model minority' thing is true. They're here for a reason!" Although mention of race or ethnicity was rare during day-to-day school life at Heathcliff, there was an outgoing Asian American youth who stirred a discussion of race during a class I observed. Ms. Lawson, a sixth-grade history teacher, started her class off one morning by asking if there were any announcements students wanted to share. One White student said it was his birthday. Alex invoked a stereotypical Asian accent and said, "Ooh, what age you turning?" The class chortled uncomfortably. "Is that how your parents talk to you?" asked Ms. Lawson. "Not at all!" Alex exclaimed. "In fact, I use that voice a lot when I want to get my way. People ask me for something and I just say, 'Sorry, no speak Engrish!'" Everyone laughed. "We could all learn a thing or two from Alex," said Ms. Lawson as the class calmed down. "Very clever. I'm sure that works on me all the time, too!" When racial meanings were invoked at Heathcliff for Asian American youth, they resonated with model minority imagery that faculty used during interviews. Other stereotypes that portrayed Asian Americans as threats, like those used at Sheldon, were incompatible with a workplace that promoted elite servitude and positioned students as achievers.

Thus far, I have described how a workplace norm among faculty that promoted servitude to students shaped teaching by positioning youth as achievers and elites. Although race operated invisibly for Heathcliff's majority of White students, teachers drew on images of Asian American students as model minorities when race became salient for this population. But where does this culture of elite servitude come from? Parents, certainly, but also from a broader set of politics that parents negotiated as they selected Heathcliff for their children and participated in its functioning. "Well, I mean, just look at the neighborhoods around here," one parent told me before a parent event, reflecting on why she sent her son to Heathcliff. "There are a lot of *bad* neighborhoods just five minutes away. At Heathcliff, you can know for sure you're sending your child to a place with other good kids."

Although Heathcliff's gates seemed to separate the school from its neighborhood, the outlying community had become much more diverse in the previous ten years. Whites remained the majority, at 76.67 percent of the population, but the size of the Latinx community had grown by 16.59 percent since 2000 to account for just over 10 percent of the total neighborhood. Despite this growth, Latinx families earned considerably less than White families. The median household income for White residents in the neighborhood was $83,246 in 2013, an increase of 26.5 percent since 2000, whereas the median household income for Latinx residents was $27,757, a decrease of 4.4 percent since 2000. Heathcliff families were likely far wealthier than the median income for Whites given the tremendous cost to attend.

Parents I spoke with at school events rarely named the racial groups they were referring to, and instead used "bad neighborhoods," "bullies," and "drug dealers" as euphemisms to allude to poor Latinx youth whom they perceived to be threats to their child's proper development. "My husband and I were so scared at the thought of sending our daughter to a public school after Heathcliff," said a parent on a panel at the school's parent event. "There's a lot of drugs and crime in the bad neighborhoods around here. We all don't want that to touch our children." Another "Heathcliff Mom" on the panel nodded in agreement. "The reality is Heathcliff is not like the rest of the world," she said. "You just have to hope that, with all that we've taught them, that they will seek out other normal kids and not be influenced by the bad ones." Parents who sent their children to Heathcliff did so to provide a "safe" environment, meaning one that separated them from the growing population of poor people of color in their community. Although parents and teachers were more willing to discuss social class than race, racial dynamics were a key facet of the Heathcliff school environment. The largely White families sent students to this school to separate them from poor students of color, especially Latinx students.[18] Their active engagement with Heathcliff faculty and staff ensured that their children got an education fit for elites. These parent-driven politics facilitated a vision of Heathcliff students as achievers in the face of poor youth of color in the outlying community. Unlike Sheldon faculty, Heathcliff faculty linked an achiever orientation to a portrayal of their Asian American students as model minorities rather than cutthroat hackers.

CONNECTING WORKPLACE CULTURE TO CLASSROOM DISCIPLINARY ORIENTATION

In previous chapters, I illustrated how schools invoked different disciplinary practices to moderate students' digital youth culture, activating kids' digital skills as cultural capital at Heathcliff Academy while portraying those same skills as threatening or irrelevant at Sheldon Junior High and César Chávez Middle School. In this chapter, I described the origins of these disciplinary orientations. I addressed this puzzle by drawing together previously disconnected literatures on colorblind racism and workplace dynamics. I argued that the predominately White, middle-class teachers in this study carry with them multiple, contradictory racialized and classed beliefs about their students of color. But I showed how teachers also interface with durable workplace cultures, variably as family-like, hostile, or compelling elite servitude. Teachers select the "appropriate" available stereotype about their students of color as it aligns with the meaning system that exists at their workplace. For White students, no such linkage occurs because Whiteness operates invisibly: White students at Sheldon avoid the hostility from teachers that students of color face, and White students at Heathcliff are simply seen as achievers.

Scholars who study organizational culture challenge education researchers to think of the classroom as shaped, in part, by norms faculty develop and share with one another. I found that teachers, especially more senior faculty who had both tenure and greater perspective on workplace dynamics, saw connections between the recent history of their school and the workplace norms that faculty, both new and more senior, had to wrestle with. Workplace norms were powerful social forces that oriented teachers to one another and to their teaching. They evoked a shared meaning system that rendered particular stereotypes teachers possessed "sensible" for that school. Table 3.1 provides a summary of this relationship between workplace dynamics and stereotype selection.

Although in the context of an interview teachers displayed awareness of multiple constructions of Asian American youth as either model minorities or cutthroat hackers raised by Tiger Moms, only teachers at Heathcliff saw their Asian American students as the former and only teachers at Sheldon saw them as the latter. Teachers at Heathcliff shared an achiever orientation to their students as a consequence of parental pressures to treat their students as elites. This orientation "fits" with the model minority imagery they described during interviews. At Sheldon, however, teachers shared a threat orientation to their students as a consequence of neighborhood demographic shifts they interpreted as a violation of their racial and social boundaries. This view of students as threats aligned with the cutthroat hacker imagery they described during interviews.

Faculty also reported a similar set of beliefs about Latinx students as either benevolent immigrants or future criminals, but only teachers at Chávez saw their Latinx students as the former and only teachers at Sheldon saw them as the latter. Teachers at Chávez shared an achiever orientation (for vocational tracks) to their students as an extension of the family-like, "in it together" mentality that carried over from the transition from an elementary school to a middle school. This achiever orientation aligned with the benevolent immigrant imagery that teachers described during interviews. At Sheldon, however,

SCHOOL	WORKPLACE NORM	ORIENTATION TO STUDENTS	ORIENTATION TO ASIANS	ORIENTATION TO LATINX	ORIENTATION TO WHITES
Cesar Chavez Middle (working-class, Latinx)	In it together	Achiever (vocational)	N/A	Benevolent immigrant	N/A
Sheldon Junior High (middle-class, Asian)	Every man for himself	Threat	Tiger Parent, cutthroat, hacker	Future gang member	Invisible
Heathcliff Academy (wealthy, White)	Serving elites	Achiever (elite)	Model minority	N/A	Invisible

TABLE 3.1: Relationship between Faculty Workplace Dynamics and Constructions of Students

the aforementioned threat orientation also applied to their Latinx students and aligned with the felonious stereotypes that teachers possessed.

An interesting consequence of the invisibility of Whiteness is how it privileged White students no matter the school context. At Heathcliff, faculty constructed White students' achievements as individual successes, whereas Asian American students' achievements were attributed to their racial group. At Sheldon, White students' invisibility shielded them from the much more visible racial statuses imposed on Asian American and Latinx students. As a consequence, Asian American and Latinx students—not Whites—became the focus of teachers' disciplinary practices to negotiate supposed threat.

Teachers' disciplinary orientations to students' digital youth culture came from how race- and class-inflected cultural stereotypes were entangled with workplace dynamics. In the next chapter, I turn to interviews with samples of eighth-grade students narrating their experiences and development over the course of middle school. These narratives illustrate how schools' different disciplinary approaches to play created students as subjects, and differently as tinkerers, rule-followers, and digital laborers.

4

SCHOOLS AS SOCIALIZING AGENTS
FOR DIGITAL PARTICIPATION

Sociologists of education who study students' cultural resources typically argue that student participation in institutionally valued activities varies by social class, resulting in unequal gains in achievement.[1] As the story goes, wealthier parents encourage their children to attend museums, follow news, politics, art, etc. These pursuits are then rewarded in institutional contexts, either by teachers who validate such participation or even by employers who seek cultural similarity.[2] But today many of these traditionally valued activities exist in digital contexts, as well. For example, children can seek out information online about news; participate in debates online related to politics and elections; create and share art of various forms online; and even learn about and access government resources, like health care information or other social services.[3] In keeping with existing scholarship, quantitative work finds that young adults exhibit class-based differences in the extent to which they pursue these types of capital-enhancing activities online.

However, the puzzle remains as to *where* children develop the skills needed to pursue such activities online. This matters because it locates a mechanism for cultural inequality in children's unequal development of resources needed to succeed. Bourdieuians typically point to parents as the source of such resources, but we know that parents, at least in this contemporary moment, are not necessarily the source of kids' digital skills.[4] If not parents, what else could drive differences in whether kids take advantage of opportunities online?

As I interviewed eighth-grade students at each of the three middle schools in this study, I started to learn that digital participation was not simply about whether students participate online but also *how*—

and further, schools played a role in shaping students' approach to online participation. For example, I asked Maggie (White, 13 years old) to describe the kinds of things she and her peers at Heathcliff Academy did online. She rolled her eyes. "Everyone here likes to make it look like they're such a big deal online, but honestly they're in eighth grade. You don't need a LinkedIn page. Who cares?" she vented. "It's a little competitive here. I mean, everyone is really smart, so they're just trying to make themselves stand out from other students and look good to teachers and colleges." As I learned about the kinds of activities that Heathcliff students pursued online, I accrued quite the cosmopolitan list of digitally blended interests: Debate. Video game development. Fan fiction book writing. Further, these edgy interests were expressed across the digital platforms used by all students in this study, like Snapchat, Instagram, YouTube, and Twitter.

In another example, Alyson, a fourteen-year-old White youth at Heathcliff, was eager to tell me her favorite things to do. "I do gymnastics and compete nationally, and I'm also really into Krav Maga right now," she said. "I use my Twitter account to share my experiences training and everything." Alyson, like other Heathcliff students, pursued a number of interests and regularly found ways to make those interests public using online platforms like Twitter. When explaining how she got started with Krav Maga and sharing her experiences online, she gestured toward her parents as a beacon of encouragement, but cited school pressures as a factor shaping her online participation:

> Well, my parents have always supported my sports, and when I found out about Krav Maga they jumped on that right away and signed me up for classes. But Twitter? Um, no. My parents know I tweet about my training but they couldn't care less, they just want me to do well in school. If I'm perfectly honest, I'm trying to look good for my school and for college. You want to stand out online, but in the right way; for the right reasons.

Alyson, like others at Heathcliff, did not go online to access news, art, or other resources cited as important in the literature. She participated online to *curate* an identity intended to make her look more worthwhile to educational institutions.

The social phenomena I analyze in the previous chapters—situated technologies, disciplining play, and workplace cultures—matter to teachers, but ultimately they create the social environment for youth. In this chapter, I focus exclusively on how young people experience these social structures. I do so by examining how these structures answer a question important to both sociologists and internet scholars: what determines whether students take advantage of resources available online? The students in this study helped me understand by flipping this question on its head: it's not just the types of digital activities kids pursue that may give them certain advantages. Schools' disciplinary orientations also play a powerful role in shaping whether students participate online in ways that may lead to unequal gains.[5] Students from Heathcliff curate a professional identity online aimed at conveying college readiness, whereas students from Chávez create and share primarily for peers, evidencing little institutionally minded savvy online. Sheldon students, meanwhile, hide their identities entirely for fear of teacher reprimand, leaving no trace of themselves for colleges or future employers aside from their school records.

Media scholars envision digital technologies as tools that provide access to an online environment rich with information and potential social capital.[6] Many of the sociological hallmarks of capital-enhancing activities—attending museums. following news, politics, and art—increasingly can be pursued online, as well. Today, by going online, youth can seek out information about news, participate in debates related to politics and elections, create and share art of various forms, and even access government resources like health care information or other social services. Additionally, they can use digital technologies to access new social environments for connecting with like-minded peers. Online affinity networks, such as those centered on an interest in a particular video game, like *Minecraft*, or even vibrant forums devoted to a particular book fandom, like *The Hunger Games*, allow people from around the world to particulate in subcultures with their own social systems. Nascent work even shows that participation in these interest-driven online networks can lead to assorted learning outcomes through forms of digital apprenticeship.[7]

Scholars who study students' online participation worry about what they call a "participation gap" that may lead to inequities.[8] As in sociological theories of cultural inequality, media scholars argue that people arrive at these information-rich online environments with an unequal distribution of cultural resources, the know-how needed to effectively navigate online contexts to their advantage. We're already seeing demographic indication of such gaps: wealthier folks are more likely than those who are financially less well-off to go online to use email, learn about stock prices and economic and political news, use search engines, and access health information; socioeconomic status and gender shape the odds that one will create and share media or information online rather than simply consume it; youth whose parents have higher levels of education are more likely to create and share media online, like music, art, or writing.[9] But what sort of online participation is it that leads to these emergent differences in capital-enhancing online behaviors?

Internet scholars refer to *networked publics* as the contemporary playing field for online participation.[10] Think back to Alyson's pursuit of competitive gymnastics. Although her training likely occurred in an athletic facility among fellow gymnasts and coaches, she used her smartphone to share images and video of her training on Twitter with any number of audiences online. "You don't really know who could see it," she said. "But you share as if the people you *need* to see it will. Like, if a college I'm applying to sees it, I want them to think that I'd be a good fit for them." "Networked publics" refers to the many, many online and offline contexts that exist and may at any point connect Alyson's gymnastics routine to other audiences. Her audience is not just those immediately around her at the athletic facility. Images or video of her routine persist as data online and are available asynchronously, potentially searchable by anyone in the world. As digital media, they can be remixed and recreated online, and it's rarely clear who is watching.

I treat here the notion of networked publics as a digitally inflected terrain upon which the students in this study differently navigate.[11] Over the course of middle school, students developed strategies for participating online that were patterned by school. While I can't link these strategies for online participation to outcomes like college admission without following these students through and after high school, I explicate existing quantitative work about the digital participation gap among young people. During interviews, students shared their digitally inflected activities that persist online, in most cases using their phones to point to their social media accounts and other digital traces, and explained how school pressures may have informed those activities. I show how teachers' approach to students' digital play influenced those students' orientation to online participation and determined whether institutions of higher education were an imagined audience online.[12]

How does disciplining play then shape online participation across networked publics? Recall in an earlier chapter that Chávez teachers disciplined play by saying that their predominately working-class, Latinx students' play was *irrelevant* to school. Teachers were not tough disciplinarians in the way that Sheldon teachers were; in fact, teachers saw each other and their students as part of a family. In turn, students processed their teachers' messages to separate play and school as well-meaning guidance to get ahead. "Teachers are worried kids will goof around if we use some of the more fun apps at school," said Anthony, a thirteen-year-old Latinx student at Chávez. "They say it's okay to communicate with others using social media, but it's not for work." As students described to me what they loved to do for fun, they began to reveal a shared boundary between "play" and "school." Teachers at each school differently established a boundary between play and school that, for Chávez youth, relegated their creativity and fun to experiences outside of school. This process of imposing boundaries upon the students is a form of school-driven, race- and class-differentiated socialization. Teacher expectations bled into students' varied practices for online participation. Because Chávez students were told that their digital play was irrelevant to learning, they pursued it online without attention to who, beyond peers, might see it. Meanwhile, Heathcliff students were building a digital resume.

CURATING EASE ONLINE AT HEATHCLIFF ACADEMY

Cordelia, a fourteen-year-old White youth at Heathcliff, was eager to tell me about her favorite thing to do. "I really, really love the *Hunger Games* series," she said. "Like, so much that I write stories about it online." I learned that Cordelia was actually a member of an online forum hosted on Wattpad.com, an online fan fiction creation community. "I don't know. I just found it and met other people who were fans just like me," she explained while pulling out her phone to show me the website. "Look, here's one of my stories." Cordelia had created what looked like a literary opus in the image of the popular book *The Hunger Games.* She described a process of writing and revision among like-minded peers in this online fan community that resulted in her getting significant accolades online for her final product. Cordelia said that her piece was featured by the website and got thousands of views. She explained how she was able to connect these online interests to her success at Heathcliff. "Yeah, the teachers and other students know about this project," she laughed. "I'm kinda seen as 'the writer' but I try not to brag too much. What's really cool is that I've gotten to submit parts of the project for class sometimes. We had this writing assignment here about morality and my teacher let me submit this instead."

At the end of the academic year, I had the pleasure of interviewing samples of eighth-grade students from a class at each school where the patterns from observation were strongest. As students shared how they processed teachers' messages about appropriate forms of digital participation, I learned of the means by which they tried to make sense of pressures from teachers, parents, and peers. Though messages from parents were largely not about technology use, they had some effect in how youth described their practices online.[13] Teachers' messages about play were particularly salient in how students described their online participation. Although Cordelia was the only fan fiction writer I spoke with at Heathcliff, each of the other students had interests that they pursued online and integrated with school success.

The eighth-grade students I interviewed at Heathcliff may have all been somewhat expert at connecting their interests to school assignments, but they said that it had taken years for them to develop a habit of integrating these interests into the classroom. For example, Tom (White, 14 years old) explained how using digital technologies in front of the whole class, like interactive whiteboards, was intimidating back when he started in fifth grade. "Teachers here really force us to get comfortable showing off our online projects to the school since we start here," he said. "It's nerve-wracking at first, but eventually you learn it's kinda fun. Teachers make you feel good for sharing your ideas." As we saw in other chapters, Heathcliff teachers disciplined play at school by requiring that students bring their peer practices online into class. "I remember it being really hard," explained Robin (White, 13 years old). "Teachers seemed to always want us to share things about ourselves and impress everyone with our assignments and really stand out. But now I can do it, easy." As part of this effort, faculty actively encouraged students to integrate media from playing online with friends into the classroom. This stood in stark contrast to the message of teachers from Chávez and Sheldon, where faculty constructed digital play as irrelevant or threatening to schooling. Heathcliff teachers' disciplinary approach was associated with students reporting play as essential to achievement in class.

An important part of Heathcliff teachers' instructional practices was to encourage youth to shine as *creative* users of technology. This often meant deferring to students' own knowledge base about the best apps to use or strategies for using technologies for different parts of daily lessons. Students explained that part of being creative with digital technology meant treating rules for school assignments as starting points for something new. For example, Ken (14 years old, White) described how he decided to replace a writing assignment with an activity in *Minecraft*:

> For class last year we had an assignment to describe city life. The assignment teachers gave us was to write a normal paper, but me and my friends were like, "Hey, let's build a city on *Minecraft*." The teacher liked our idea and *loved* the finished product, it turned out really well. I ended up being able to use *Minecraft* for class. Teachers may not understand it but they let us bring stuff like that in. *Minecraft* is after all a creativity game.

Ken's teacher may not have fully grasped *Minecraft* but allowed him to use the game in class to enhance his learning experience. On one hand, this was an example of Heathcliff faculty activating a student's digital interest as cultural capital for achievement. On the other, as Ken reported, it was a message to him that he had some ownership over his own class activities.

Heathcliff students described, over and over, how sharing their creative digital expressions in class was a legitimizing experience that gave them authority over their own curriculum. For example, Rupert (White, 13 years old) was "really into history," so much so that he devoted a lot of time on Instagram and Reddit (an online forum) to sharing things he learned about civil wars around the world. "Yeah, I mean, it's just something I've always been into," he said. "But Mr. Filippo [social studies] always has me go up and share what I'm working on to the class. Like for one of our projects, he actually just let me submit something I was working on for Reddit about the Crimean war. He's cool like that." Teachers' disciplinary orientation to play positioned these types of creative expressions online as valuable to school. "One of the best things about Heathcliff is that you kinda learn over the years to think about what *you* want to do," reflected Cordelia (White, 14 years old). "I remember being so insecure when I was in fifth grade. Now I see teachers as my friends, and whatever I share I know they'll help find a way to make it matter." Students came to see school assignments as encouragement to come up with new and exciting projects.

Inside and outside of school, students at Heathcliff shared many of the same interests as Chávez and Sheldon youth did, including video games, reading e-books, and using social media, but they emphasized their interests in specific creative genres that blended their pursuits with an online presence. For example, Tom (White, 14 years old) shared his love for debate. "I've been debating for a few years now," he said. "I want to be humble but I've become quite good at it. I have a YouTube account where I give advice to other debaters so they can get better, too." Robin (White, 13 years old) told me about her passion for platform diving. "I always try to have someone take photos of my dive; it's basically my entire Instagram," she laughed. "I really like movement in general, it's why I love sports and diving." Heathcliff students enjoyed playing online using similar tools and platforms as Chávez and Sheldon youth, but they also pursued a number of atypical interests and shared those activities using their social media accounts. In explaining why and how they pursued these interests online, students cited their parents as sources of encouragement for the interest, but their teachers as a reason why they curated themselves online the way they did.

As I spoke with Heathcliff students, I found that they maintained highly visible online presences using various social media. Only one Heathcliff student locked some of her online accounts, citing her parents' worries about strangers. Heathcliff youth described an online curation approach with the intent to appease institutional authorities and convey a sense of expertise and ease to others who saw them online. "I mean, we all know that at the end of the day it doesn't matter if some girl thinks a picture you put up is weird," explained Cordelia (White, 14 years old). "Before I put something up online, I always think about if a teacher or colleges see it. I try to make sure they'd like what they see." Heathcliff students' curatorial practices emphasized creating and sharing acceptable media online rather than minimizing their digital footprints altogether. "Getting good grades is just the first step of doing well here," said Nathan (White, 14 years old). "There's a lot of pressure to act as if you're like the next top 'this' or 'that.' It feels like you won't get into college unless you're a really good student and you have a million Twitter followers, too."

I see close connections between Heathcliff students' reflections on their online participation and how Shamus Khan described the "performance of ease" among the elite private school students in his study.[14] Khan described ease as a way for elite students to convey fluency in both high and low culture and demonstrate excellence at difficult tasks while making the execution look easy. The work that this does, Khan argues, is to obscure inequities by making the student's success appear natural to them. I find that the private school youth in the present study appear to be developing and extending this performance of ease online. As mentioned, they pursued interests similar to those of students I interviewed at Chávez and Sheldon: they used Snapchat, Instagram, and/or Twitter to hang out with friends and create and share media online. But Heathcliff youth did more, pursuing diverse interests (Krav Maga, competitive gymnastics, fan fiction, etc.) and gaining attention and accolades from networked publics online. While it takes a great deal of work to curate these presences online, students wanted to make it look easy. "You just want to make sure you look like you 'get it,'" explained Nathan (14 years old, White). "It's actually a lot of work to make sure you look good online. It's like you have to think about it every time you take a photo and put it up there." Heathcliff students privately described their online curation as requiring a lot of effort, but dichotomously characterized it as "fun" and not a big deal. Heathcliff students explained that they cared less about their peers seeing them online than they did about teachers and future college officials. But it is possible that Heathcliff youth diminished the importance of peers as a means to assert a performance of ease at school, since in interviews they stated that it took a great deal of work to, at the very least, maintain an online presence. Heathcliff youth maintained highly visible online presences and curated their media to appear special and worthwhile in the eyes of teachers and college admissions officers.

DIGITAL LABOR AT CÉSAR CHÁVEZ MIDDLE SCHOOL

> I love music. So me and my brother, we take our favorite
> music and make something new with it. He'll have an idea for
> different sounds to add, and I'll add the beats. He's really good
> at thinking which songs could go together, and I'm good at
> actually remixing it. We do this for fun whenever we're not at
> school or not doing homework.

Bailey (14 years old, Latinx), a student at César Chávez Middle School, was obsessed with making music with her brother using her computer. She and her brother maintained an account on SoundCloud, a popular music-sharing app, where their songs were shared online for others to leave comments and make suggestions for new tracks. Bailey pursued her interests with others using various digital tools. Bailey's interest-driven activities meet many of the hallmarks advocated by twenty-first-century approaches to learning online. She learned how to use editing software to create and remix audio files. She navigated networked publics to share her music and get feedback. But when I asked her about integrating this work with school, she laughed. "Teachers wouldn't get it . . . and if I shared it with them they'd probably find a way to not make it as much fun anymore."

Like Bailey, the Chávez students I interviewed also reported having a lot of fun with digital technologies *outside* of school. They reveled in that moment when the school bell rang and they were free to go have fun. "I can't wait until the school day is over so I can go home and play GTA [Grand Theft Auto] with my friends," said Anthony (Latinx, 13 years old), a student at Chávez. "I play socially, like online with other people, mostly people from school, and I stick with my friends in a party." Caleb (Latinx, 13 years old) said that he loved to hang out with his friends at the park, and when he was not outside, he loved listening to music. "I follow a lot of music online, either on YouTube or other apps," he said. "It's a nice break from homework or just to relax after a long day at school." In addition to gaming and music, youth also enjoyed reading on their phones. "I read something like a book a week," Summer (Latinx, 14 years old) told me. "I can download them from the local library to my phone. What's funny is that I read much more of this than I do stuff for school. It's just more fun." As students described to me what they loved to do for fun, they began to reveal a shared boundary between "play" and "school." For these students, part of what made an activity playful and enjoyable was that it was *not* associated with school.

If a learning scientist were to survey students about their digital activities in both Heathcliff and Chávez, they would observe similar patterns exhibiting digital literacies learned through online activities. Students from both schools pursued interests online, and in doing so learned how to communicate with others online and become sophisticated with digital tools so that they could create and share new media. What these learning scientists would miss, however, is the role that institutions have in constructing the value of these technologies in school. Teachers at each school differently established a boundary between play and school that, for Chávez youth, relegated their creativity and fun to zones outside of educational institutions.

The way I began unpacking this was by asking Chávez students what it was about school, and particularly digital technology use while at school, that they found so unappealing. "I don't know. Teachers would make it not fun," sighed Richard (14 years old, Latinx). "Like

I'm trying to imagine bringing my [Nintendo] DS in. They'd just tell me to save it for home because it's distracting from work." Some students, like Richard, shared that teachers would see digital play—and video games, in particular—as distinctly separate from schoolwork. But others said that teachers would make it less fun. "I mean honestly, Matt, they'd just kill it," Summer (14 years old, Latinx) laid out for me. "I mean, what do you think Mr. Weber would do if I told him I like to read books online for fun? He'd make me write a paper about it, I swear." Summer's comments echoed other Chávez youth when I pressed them to share what would happen if they brought what they liked to do for fun to school. The sentiment was that play would count as achievement only if it were no longer play.

Recall in an earlier chapter that Chávez teachers disciplined play by saying that play was irrelevant to school. Teachers at Chávez were not tough disciplinarians in the way that Sheldon teachers were; in fact, teachers saw each other and their students as part of a paternalistic family. In turn, students processed teachers' messages to separate play and school as well-meaning guidance to get ahead. Students saw their digital styles as irrelevant to school, and correspondingly created a division between their interest-driven activities and schooling. "Social media is fun, but school isn't open to it because people take advantage of it and mess around with it," said Juliet (13 years old, Latinx). "Messing around isn't productive." Students at Chávez came to think of the fun types of messing around on digital platforms as separate from work. If Mizuko Ito, Sonja Baumer, Matteo Bittanti, et al. are correct that "messing around" with digital technology is a key part of developing affinity for creative production, then Chávez students were missing out on that opportunity in school.[15] Although Chávez students had the potential to meaningfully integrate their digital play into learning at school, the paternalistic ethos of Chávez faculty imposed a deficit frame on the value of their students' digital play.[16] Moreover, Chávez faculty imposed on students a division between work and play that functioned to relegate their own agentic impulses to time *outside* of school.

As at Heathcliff, there were very few observed or reported examples of teacher-imposed penalties on students for misbehavior. Chávez students did, however, describe some disciplinary action teachers would pursue if fun uses of digital tools surfaced too much in class. "We do have a phone box at the office," Seth (13 years old, Latinx) told me. "It's kind of a joke, though. Most students aren't really that bad, but if someone is really going out of their way to game during class, their phone is sent to the office and they pick it up at the end of the day." Kendra laughed at mention of the "phone box." "Teachers sometimes bring up the phone box as a joke," she said. "It's usually just a nice reminder that we shouldn't be talking that much and focus on work." Chávez students generally described teachers' disciplinary approach to digital play as a polite, but persistent, pressure that teachers imposed during day-to-day instruction.

When explaining the value of digital technologies for school and how it might relate to their future, students framed such uses through a lens of productive, yet laborious, work. "We use things like Microsoft Word and Keynote so that we can get better at taking notes and stuff," explained Riley (Latinx, 13 years old). "It will probably help me get a job or a career. It's about getting the right skills for it." Most students emphasized that uses of digital technology at school were tied to developing skills for a job someday. "Typing is important," said Mercedes (Latinx, 13 years old). "It helps when you need to search for big words to put in a paper or something. I'm sure I'll need that for high school or a job." Kendra (Latinx, 14 years old) also saw digital technology use at school as valuable for work. "Using computers and iPads and stuff are good because it's helping us get ready for high school and college," she said. "Like even sometimes you have to contact people with technology and search for things." As a consequence of the faculty-imposed boundary between play and school, Chávez youth saw the digital technology used in school settings as a tool for labor.

As I learned more about how Chávez students pursued their interests outside of school, I noticed differences from Heathcliff youth in both form and style. Chávez students overlapped with Heathcliff students in some ways, notably in their interests in music, video games, using social media, and in reading online books. But Chávez students did not also pursue more eccentric interests like Krav Maga or more institutionally salient tastes like competitive debate or gymnastics. These differences in content could be attributed to Heathcliff parents' coaching their children for distinction. But how Chávez and Heathcliff students curated their interests online differed considerably. Whereas

Heathcliff students cited teachers and future colleges as audiences for their digital footprints, Chávez students reported curating their online presence with a mind to their peer groups. For example, Juliet (Latinx, 13 years old) explained that she did not worry much about who would see her information online, with the exception of her girlfriends. "I don't really worry about who will see my data," she explained. "It's more that certain people I know don't see stuff I don't want. So I only keep tweets or pictures up that my friends wouldn't give me a hard time about." Graham (Asian, 14 years old) also described curating his online presence with respect to his peers. "I don't share stuff to Facebook because I don't want people there to see it. I'll share that stuff instead to specific friends on Kik rather than the whole world on Facebook. That would be embarrassing." Some Chávez students also curated their image online with a mind to peers in online affinity networks they participated in. "Yeah, I mean my entire Twitter account is basically me promoting the music I make that I share on SoundCloud," explained Bailey. "It's all tweets about my music, or to other people who I like who make music, too." Bailey, like some others I interviewed, curated her social presence online primarily for peers who created music—not teachers or college officials.

When asked about other, nonpeer entities who might view their online activities, Chávez youth typically said they did not care. They referenced their teachers' blasé approach to their online presence. Students rarely said that they worried about what teachers, parents, or other adults with authority might think about what they shared online. For example, Hank (Asian, 14 years old) said that he used Instagram a lot and played games that shared posts online about his activities. He shrugged when I asked about what his parents or teachers might think if they saw his online data. "My parents don't really care what I do online, as long as I don't get into trouble," he explained. "And I don't really care if my teachers see it. They might think it's silly but they really wouldn't care." Kendra (Latinx, 14 years old) also cared little about who would see her online presence beyond her friend groups. "I don't care about who sees it. I don't worry about my teachers or even companies looking at my stuff because I have no reason to worry," she said. "I don't use it in wrong ways." Bailey (14 years old, Latinx) similarly had a nonchalant attitude toward how her data might be used beyond her immediate friends. "I don't really worry about the government or companies because I feel like they're going to use it anyway," she said. "And teachers don't care, unless you do something really bad online like bully someone. I mostly just don't want to look embarrassing to my friends," she laughed. Students at Chávez were concerned with curating their digital footprints for local peer networks. When asked about other entities that might view their presence, they said that teachers would not care.

Teachers at Chávez disciplined students' play by communicating to youth that what they did online for fun was irrelevant to learning. Instead, they prioritized using digital technologies at school to teach basic skills in typing, presentations, online research, and programming. As a consequence, youth reported that digital technology use at school was important but laborious, and devoid of the fun and creative activities they pursue outside of school with peers. The potential impact of this becomes more apparent as these students' accounts are compared to stories told by Heathcliff students about their digital curation efforts. Heathcliff and Chávez youth overlapped on a number of digital interests, like using social media and playing video games. But Heathcliff students also pursued interests intended to distinguish them, like competitive debate or sports. What's more, Heathcliff youth curated these interests online in ways that they hoped would impress teachers and college officials. Chávez youth did not. Thus, kids' digital footprints varied by school in ways that were shaped by how teachers constructed the value of kids' play at school.

While it is beyond the scope of this study to document how college officials might differently consider kids' digital footprints, it is certainly within our purview to reflect on how kids' consciousness is affected by how play and work are constructed at school. The sociology of education is in many ways founded on theories of school socialization that point to the role teacher messaging has on student consciousness as a mechanism for later inequality. As the argument goes, schools serving wealthier students coach them into a manager mindset, while schools serving less-privileged children impose worker-bee mindsets in their students. What I clarify in this chapter is that student consciousness is actually shaped by teachers injecting different assumptions about the relationship between play and work. Heathcliff youth see play and institutional success as inseparable: their creative selfhood is fused with doing well at school. Chávez youth, meanwhile, learn to separate school from fun, relegating their creative efforts to activities that will not help them climb the institutional ladder.

GHOSTING AT SHELDON JUNIOR HIGH

"Want me to show you?" Harry (14 years old, Asian) smirked as he opened his school Chromebook and turned it around for me to see. He had just recounted for me a handful of stories about other students getting in trouble for "messing around" online by sending messages to one another. When I asked him how students tried to avoid getting caught, he described something called "ghosting":

> There's apps you can get on your phone or even use on the
> Chromebooks that let you ghost. Ghosting is like, you can
> hide from teachers online. See, I open an app in the browser
> that makes it so they can't track that it's me. Now I could use a
> website to chat with my friends and not get caught. I won't
> say that I've ever done it, but . . . [*laughter*].

It was no secret to Sheldon students that their teachers were tough disciplinarians. In interviews, students all recounted examples similar to what I observed in classes: teachers regularly disciplined kids' digital play, like communicating online or creating and sharing new media, by positioning these activities as threatening to learning. But while Heathcliff and Chávez youth were largely aligned with teacher expectations, there was considerably more student resistance at Sheldon. One way students resisted was by ghosting, or evading the school's means to surveil students online.

Like Chávez youth, Sheldon students also enjoyed a number of different online activities with friends, but they pursued them outside of school. The activities students reported were very similar to those detailed by students at the other schools, like playing video games with friends, reading books using their smartphones, using Instagram, or following Tumblr accounts. But Sheldon students said that the reason why they largely pursued these activities outside of school was that they feared the consequences of getting caught. Students at Sheldon generally saw their teachers as tough disciplinarians and viewed their own digital play at school as risk-laden. For example, Anne (15 years old, Asian) described teachers at Sheldon as "not so nice" and explained that "teachers say social media is harmful." Anne saw her own social media use as "just for fun with friends" but noted that she "would never use it at school because teachers watch what you do online." Teachers' disciplinary practices had the effect of turning work and play into a binary for students, and this binary was so rigid that students like Anne maintained a low profile online at school to avoid punishment.

Most students cited their first year at Sheldon as an important period when they learned that play online and work must be separated while at school. "I mean, before I started at Sheldon I would just use Facebook or whatever with friends," explained Charisma (14 years old, Asian). "Nobody really cared at our old school. At Sheldon, the first thing they did was take us to a big meeting and force us to sign letters saying we won't use our phones at school." Unlike Chávez, Sheldon had no "phone box." "iPhones just aren't allowed at all," said Armin (14 years old, Latinx). "If they catch you with it out in the hallways or in class you're done for. You'll get a detention." In the previous academic year, the school had suspended twenty-seven students, mostly for technology use that violated school policy. "I'll never forget the first time they printed out my messages," recounted Quentin (14 years old, Asian). "Mr. Lenk printed my messages to a friend of mine I did while at school and I had no idea he could see it. Then he showed it to the whole class." Students explained that they learned that using technology at school was threatening only as a result of teacher action over the course of their four years at school. As at Chávez and Heathcliff, teacher disciplinary approaches to digital play had the effect of shaping kids' approach to technology use at school. Sheldon students learned that school was not the appropriate setting for online play and dreaded consequences like public embarrassment and other punishments.

Gender and race were reflected in students' stories about their digital pursuits much more at Sheldon than at the other schools in this study. For the young women I interviewed, keeping a "low pro-file" at Sheldon meant complying with teacher demands not to use digital technology at school for fun.[17] Some of the young men I spoke with, however, cited ghosting online as a means to resist unrealistic teacher demands. "I mean, teachers just take it too far," said Wesley (14 years old, Asian). "Like they get upset at us, but most of them barely even know how to use a computer. It's almost like they're ask-ing for kids to mess around." Although a handful of young women also said that teachers' expectations were unfair, only the young men described taking action to resist teacher expectations. "I know the guy who hacked the teacher website last year, was the funniest thing I've ever seen," said Harry (14 years old, Asian). "Teachers like not helping us when we ask questions about assignments and tell us to go to their website instead. Well, someone did!" When asked about why young men tended to ghost or hack accounts, some of the students pointed to race and gender stereotypes. "I mean, they say Asians are good at technology, and I guess if you piss an Asian guy off, that's how he fights back," said Quentin (14 years old, Asian).[18]

Not only was there more resistance to teacher expectations, but students also shared more stories of peer harassment at Sheldon than students reported at other schools. "There's signs everywhere that are like 'no bullying,' but there's a lot of drama here," Marc (13 years old, Latinx) told me. "I feel like every day you hear about someone getting called out on Snap[chat] from a kid in another class." Recall that in the previous chapter, Sheldon teachers reported a hostile faculty en-vironment, and those messages of hostility translated into the class-room. Race again crept into how students reflected on peer dramas. "A lot of times it's Asians vs. Latinos," said Charisma (14 years old, Asian). "They [Latinx students] just tend to pick a lot of the fights." Asian American students who made this claim referred to aspects of the troublemaker stereotype as a justification. In separate inter-views, however, Latinx students shared the same sentiment about their Asian counterparts. This illustrates yet another complication of teachers' racial stereotyping of students of color: Sheldon teachers facilitated hostility in the classroom by drawing on racial stereotypes to justify their belief that student online activities were threatening to learning.[19]

Students shared that a related effect of teachers' construction of online activities as threat was that students kept a low profile online, especially when harassing other students. "What really stinks, now that I think about it, is that when people say mean stuff to other students it's not easy to find them," explained Amber (14 years old, Asian), referring to students' messages from ghost accounts. "Teachers don't want us to do stuff online and so students hide online, but then if something bad happens teachers don't know who did it or how to help." Students referred to digital contexts at school as threatening environments where the best strategy to get by—in the face of either possible sanctions by teachers or harassment from peers—was to maintain a low profile online.

When I asked Sheldon students what mattered to achieve at school, most cited doing well on tests or getting good grades. "I mean, my parents do want me to do well overall, but teachers just expect you to do well on tests," said Emma (13 years old, Asian). "That's what will help get into a good college someday." Sheldon students did not see digital technology use at school as really that valuable for learning. This stands in contrast with Chávez youth, who believed digital technology use at school was important, albeit laborious. Instead, students at Sheldon said technology skills were good to have, but secondary to getting good grades and doing well on tests. "Technology is getting more advanced these days. It's helpful to stay on top of it," Amber (Asian, 14 years old) explained. "But at the end of the day I have to get good grades to get into a good college." Daniel (15 years old, Asian) said that "school is a stepping-stone to get to the right place, it's not where I have fun. I save *Minecraft* for home." Sheldon youth reported that digital technology use was not directly related to achieving in school, and instead cited doing well according to other metrics teachers positioned as more central to their achievement. For example, Michelle (13 years old, Asian) explained that "Instagram is cool and everything, but what's going to help me get into college is to do well on the tests they give us in class. School is kind of like a game in that way, to figure out how to do well. Getting the best grades you can is like a race." Students at Sheldon positioned getting into a good college as a primary objective, and neither digital skills nor play online was seen as a key element of the college preparation process.

Instead, students conformed to standards of achievement that teachers created in their classrooms, such as getting A's on exams.

While Heathcliff and Chávez youth were taught to see particular uses of technology as conducive to achievement, Sheldon students saw technology as unimportant to school performance. Teachers' disciplinary approach to play—that digital play is threatening to learning—was responded to by students variably with complicity and resistance. Whether students resisted teachers by ghosting online or instead complied with these standards, the reported effect was the same: students perceived digital play at school as ultimately unhelpful to achievement. Some male students I interviewed focused their creativity toward means to resist teacher expectations, but most young men and women at Sheldon instead saved play for outside of school. However, a curious pattern emerged when I learned more about how they actually pursued their interests.

Remember that Heathcliff youth curated online interests to impress teachers and future colleges, and Chávez youth curated online interests to impress their peers and their interest-driven online communities. When I interviewed Sheldon youth about their interests, I found that they were the only students who said that they preferred to *consume* media across these digital platforms rather than actively create media to share widely with others. For example, Anne (Asian, 15 years old) explained that she followed others on social media but she did not produce her own media to share. "I use Twitter to follow celebrities, YouTube to watch videos, but I don't share much on Twitter," she said. "I just don't have anything interesting to say!" Elizabeth (Asian, 13 years old) said that she did like to share things online but did it only through restricted channels. "I have an Instagram and sometimes post things there, but it's completely locked down and only certain friends can see it," she said. Only one Chávez student blocked their social media accounts from public access. Every Sheldon student with the exception of two youth restricted their accounts to prevent people from seeing them. This striking difference suggested that even though both Chávez and Sheldon students pursued play outside of school, Sheldon students' play online, even outside of school, occurred in closely guarded settings.

I asked Sheldon students why they either did not create media online or restricted who could see their online activities. In addition to peer pressures, they worried a great deal about authorities from educational institutions finding them online. "I definitely don't share things on Facebook because my friends would think I'm a weirdo," said Quentin (Asian, 14 years old). "But I lock my Twitter account because if a teacher finds me, that would be really bad." Elizabeth (Asian, 13 years old) worried that if teachers found her Instagram they would suspect her of not doing her schoolwork. "My parents are pretty chill, but if my teacher found my Instagram she might think that I was using it instead of doing my work," she said. "I've heard of other students getting in trouble for using it during class, even if they only posted something between classes or after school. I'm not taking that risk." A number of students extended their fears of being caught online to college admissions, as well. "I don't want a college to search for me online and find out that I play Candy Crush or anything else," explained Wesley (Asian, 14 years old). "It's better that they don't see anything about me online and just focus on my grades and the rest of my application." Not only did Sheldon youth separate play from schoolwork, they carefully minimized their digital footprint out of fear of retribution from school authorities and even future colleges.

DIGITAL PLAY, SCHOOL BOUNDARIES, AND STUDENT ONLINE PARTICIPATION

In this chapter I showed how social forces at school, in the form of teachers' disciplinary approach to play, shaped how students imagined digital activities in and outside of school (see table 4.1). Faculty at Heathcliff Academy encouraged students to merge their play online with classroom lessons. Heathcliff students described how they used classroom assignments as starting points to make something new, like a *Minecraft* creation or online creative writing, in order to do well. Students thus saw their digital play as essential to learning and took pride in sharing their online interests in class. Teachers at César Chávez Middle School communicated to students that their digital play was irrelevant to schooling. As a result, students relegated their creative impulses to digital activities outside of school, and they thought of their in-school tasks of typing, programming, and presentations as boring, albeit important, labor. Because teachers at Sheldon Junior High construed students' digital play as threatening to learning, these youth saved play for outside of school, as well. But while Chávez students saw (boring) digital skills as important for achievement, Sheldon students believed digital skills were of secondary importance to their performance on exams.

These varied student orientations had an impact on how students interacted in online publics, in ways that may shape their later life opportunities. I found that teachers' disciplinary approaches toward play shaped how students curated media that came to represent them online. Sheldon youth, out of fear of teacher retribution for messing around online, highly restricted their online presence. They did not become adept at creating and sharing media in highly visible settings online. Chávez youth did get quite good at creating and sharing media online. But because they believed teachers did not care about what they did online, they created online media only with mind to their peers. Heathcliff students, too, practiced creating and sharing online, but they developed highly curated online presences to appease institutional authorities. They pursued their interests visibly online in order to appear as good candidates for later educational success, like college admissions.

These data implicate teachers in a school process that differently guides students into strategies for navigating networked publics online. Sociologists and internet scholars may both worry that students may differently take advantage of the informational and social opportunities, like news, learning materials, government information, art, and other resources increasingly made available online. This study shows that schools don't just have a hand in shaping whether children participate online. They communicate different expectations about *how* children should participate. Here, media scholars' treatment of the digital sphere as part of a networked public—or a stage with many potential audiences, including not only peers but also future employers—is helpful in understanding how students are differently learning to participate online in ways that may be capital-enhancing. Although family and peers likely have an impact on the specific interests

SCHOOL	DISCIPLINARY APPROACH	STUDENT ORIENTATION	STUDENT ONLINE BEHAVIOR
Cesar Chavez Middle (working-class, Latinx)	Play is irrelevant to school	Students pursue play outside of school and see school as a place for laborious digital work	Highly visible online, create and share media curated for peers
Sheldon Junior High (middle-class, Asian)	Play is threatening to school	Students pursue play outside of school and see exams and grades as more important for achievement than digital skills	Restricted online presence to avoid teacher punishment, mostly consume rather than create and share media
Heathcliff Academy (wealthy, White)	Play is essential to school	Students pursue play at school and use school rules as starting points for creative expression	Highly visible online, create and share media curated for teachers and college admissions officers

TABLE 4.1: Relationship between Teacher Discipline and Student Online Participation

students pursue, online and offline, teachers coach students' digital participation and how they navigate networked publics. Heathcliff students interpreted teacher messages about the tremendous educational value of their digital play by curating online identities not unlike digital resumes for future colleges and jobs. Other students did not.

CONCLUSION

Digital tools are often designed to be employed in particular ways, but the people who ultimately use them remind me that local contexts aid in interpreting their value. These interpretations do the work of embedding digital technologies into the social fabric of schools, with the result that various hardware and software are applied in ways far beyond their intended uses.

There's no clearer way to observe the power of such interpretations than through comparison. Take *Minecraft*, a video game popular with many students at the time of this study. At Heathcliff Academy, a private middle school serving mostly wealthy and White students, teachers saw *Minecraft* and other forms of kids' digital play as *essential* to learning. Faculty cited the digital know-how associated with gameplay—seeing parallels to architecture, urban planning, project management, and creativity—as valuable to education in the twenty-first century. They would even allow students to replace some class assignments with projects created in the game.

Just a forty-minute drive away, teachers at Sheldon Junior High perceived *Minecraft* and other video games as sending an entirely different signal about their students. At this school, where the student body was primarily middle-class and Asian American, the notion that *Minecraft* could be educational was a joke. Teachers variously described video games like *Minecraft* as "garbage," subject to student abuse, or otherwise *threatening* to learning. At Sheldon, digital tools were helpful only insofar as they made it easier to accomplish "traditional" educational outcomes measured by exams.

The final school in this study took a third approach. The predominantly working-class and Latinx student body at César Chávez Middle School also played video games like *Minecraft*, but teachers there . . .

didn't really care. While they recognized that students had social lives outside of school, the faculty perceived themselves as responsible for guiding students toward working-class digital jobs. In this sense, digital play in games like *Minecraft* was *irrelevant* to school. Teachers dismissed the value of gaming in favor of teaching basic skills in coding, website-making, and word processing. Chávez faculty saw creative play in games like *Minecraft* as fun for outside of school but viewed the rote digital skills taught in class as truly educational.

These interpretative differences unearthed by school comparison reveal a major barrier to the learning agenda currently advocated by educational scholarship and contemporary education technology reform initiatives. Specifically, research on "new literacies" argues that youth and young adults, the earliest adopters of hardware like smartphones and software like social media applications, learn important skills through digital play with friends. Young people hang out, mess around, and "geek out" as they play with friends online.[1] In the process, they develop facility with online communication and collaboration, as well as the tools needed to create and share new media online. These skills, scholars argue, are valuable with respect to learning outcomes and for enhancing students' potential in our changing labor market. Why is it that faculty at a school serving wealthy and White students imagined the value of digital play in a game like *Minecraft* in the image that this scholarship describes, whereas faculty at the other two schools did not?

This question is particularly important to sociologists because it exposes a twist in our current thinking about cultural inequality in education. I write this book at an interesting point in history. Young people are more adept at using this era's technologies for production than most of their parents and teachers. Such a circumstance presents unique opportunity to ameliorate educational inequality spurred by children's unequal acquisition of valued cultural resources, like digital know-how. Scholars of educational inequality typically point to children's unequal childhoods to explain class-based differences in achievement at school.[2] At the time of this study, though, young people arrived at school with a similar baseline set of digital skills from play online with peers. If youth, regardless of social origin, share similar valued competencies, then underserved youth may finally make strides in their climb up the opportunity structure in education. This is, in fact, the possibility offered to us by theories of cultural mobility: if we could only close gaps in valued cultural know-how driven by unequal childhoods, then we would see working-class children finally make strides.[3]

The students that I profiled in the previous chapter suggest that kids' potential as budding technologists gets bifurcated as they pass through middle school. Despite the fact that digital play with peers led to the development of digital skills with online communication, media editing and production, and even the basics of programming logic, these eighth-graders reported different conceptions of whether online play was acceptable or even welcome in schools. While students at a school for mostly White and wealthy youth came to see digital play, including social media and video games, as fun and even necessary to achievement, students at schools serving less privileged and mostly students of color were taught that play at school was either irrelevant or threatening to schooling. Schools differently disciplined digital play, and in doing so, they differently shaped how young people came to evaluate their own digital self-worth in these settings.

Sociologists have tended to ignore the processes by which digital technologies and their users are constructed.[4] Reformers, too, paint the introduction of digital technologies in schools and among young people more generally as causal mechanisms for particular outcomes.[5] They have not well considered how social forces at school shape the way teachers and students imagine the value of technology and what counts as its successful use. In my fieldwork, I observed how teachers differently conceived of very similar digital technologies as productive portals into young people's lives, tools for surveillance and punishment, or platforms for rote digital labor. This occurred despite school-level closures in digital access gaps.

In this book, I unpack both *how* and *why* teachers conceive of digital technologies and their students' use of them in such different ways, so that we can begin to think more critically about our methods to ensure that schools provide opportunity for upward mobility rather than create additional setbacks. Comparing educational institutions where school-level digital divides have closed helps us to uncover what blockages to student achievement might exist despite these reform efforts. Contrasting schools serving populations that differ in class and race, key sociological predictors of student outcomes, allows us to be mindful of the interaction of student status with digital pedagogy. Permit me to begin this chapter by reviewing the story I've told about education and digital youth as evidenced by this comparative methodological approach. Then I will discuss the implications of the mechanism described in this book, namely, how race and class factor into perceptions of students' academic and creative self-worth, online and offline.

SITUATING EDUCATIONAL TECHNOLOGIES AT CHÁVEZ, SHELDON, AND HEATHCLIFF

Although I selected the schools for this study because they each had similar, high-quality technologies at their disposal, I was struck by how differently school members imagined the value of digital technologies. César Chávez Middle School (serving mostly working-class Latinx students) and Heathcliff Academy (serving mostly wealthy White students) not only had access to similar high-quality education technologies, but also shared pedagogical commitments to teaching digital skills like information searching, website creation, and programming. If a learning scientist were to survey teachers and students at both schools, they would find that school-level gaps in technology availability and digitally minded instruction were seemingly closed despite racial-ethnic and class differences in their student demographics.

Ethnographic data can do the work of documenting the day-to-day uses and interpretations of digital tools just beneath the surface of both digital access and stated pedagogical commitments. Despite the aforementioned similarities in digital access and pedagogy, Heathcliff faculty saw digital technologies as productive *portals* into young people's lives at home and among peers, encouraging students to use iPads and other tools to take photos, record video, and bring creations from their online participation to the classroom as part of a learning process. Chávez teachers instead saw digital technologies as valuable insofar as they helped to teach rote skills for technical jobs. While Heathcliff teachers used digital technologies as artifacts that blended family and peer lives with school for learning, Chávez faculty imagined digital technologies as practice for a digitized factory shop floor. Further, the work that this basic skills discourse did was impose a top-down model of teacher-student learning; rather than seeing technologies as "portals" that treat what students do at home and with friends as having educational potential, Chávez cut those opportunities off in favor of less engaging and even paternalistic instruction.

Sheldon Junior High (serving mostly middle-class Asian American students) had different types of digital technologies than Heathcliff or Chávez, and I found out that they intentionally purchased different tools because they sought to construct a teaching environment that was armed for surveillance. Faculty and administrators used tools like Chromebooks, Wi-Fi controls, and cloud-based applications like Google Drive to monitor not just student activities but also other faculty. Teachers used these tools to police students for various types of online behavior, like texting, playing games, and watching YouTube. Interestingly, these "bad" behaviors at Sheldon were treated as educationally valuable at Heathcliff.

These findings stand in stark contrast to technologically determinist thinking, or work that argues that technologies have independent effects on their users.[6] It's neither the mere availability of digital technologies nor monolithic student states like "screen time" that directly lead to particular outcomes. Rather, conversations with teachers revealed a more nuanced dialectic relationship: people adopt technologies in different ways as a consequence of their social environment. In some cases, the technologies that administrators purchased differed from school to school because of these local, human factors. This way of thinking is much more in line with social theorists' call for a relational approach to understanding technology.[7] Further, by fleshing out how school members differently construct the value of digital technologies, we can then identify the processes that may shape day-to-day instructional practice.

DISCIPLINING PLAY

A central focus of this book was to understand what teachers did with students' digital know-how: did they treat the digital skills these kids learned from play as a resource to help students do well in class and get better grades? Education reforms citing the value of these digital skills would say so. Sociologists of cultural stratification in schools would say so, too. Even though students varied by race-ethnicity and class at each school, they possessed similar, valued cultural resources in the form of digital skills. According to the prevailing logic, this would circumvent inequities caused by their having arrived at school with different resources. Digital skills could be a resource that teachers activate in the classroom to help kids get ahead, a resource referred to by sociologists as cultural capital. Indeed, I find that teachers transformed kids' digital play into cultural capital.[8] But whether teachers did this or not depended on the school.

My first task in examining how teachers treat kids' digital knowledge in school was to evaluate the extent to which students in these schools reflected national data on technology adoption among kids. Consistent with existing research, I found that the sampled youth in this study possessed a similar baseline of cultural resources in the form of digital know-how. Digital divides were, as national reports suggest, minimal when it came to access to technologies needed to play online with friends.[9] Nearly all children regularly used smartphones, iPads, laptops, and internet-connected video game systems. Some students at César Chávez Middle School did not own as many high-quality digital technologies as students at other schools, but they all had access to a combination of the aforementioned devices such that they regularly played online with friends.[10] Regardless of social origin, the youth in this study all shared similar interests in social media use, video games, online reading and writing, and image and video making. Incidentally, to pursue those interests with their friends, they had to develop facility with various digital technologies and online software. These youth did not learn this facility from their parents. In fact, students treated the notion that their parents could have helped them learn digital skills as a joke.

I use the term "discipline" to help articulate the process by which teachers transform play—the source of kids' digital skills in this study— into cultural capital for achievement.[11] Many of us probably think of "discipline" as corrective punishment in the classroom. The term has another meaning, one that has been used by classic social reproduction theories in education. Michel Foucault's famous (albeit grimly articulated) explanation of "discipline" rests on a story of how power is asserted in modern society.[12] Back in the day of monarchs and lords, he argues, leaders used brute force to control people. Today we use methods that are far less gruesome and exert power in more subtle ways. We leverage the organization of institutions, like militaries, hospitals, or schools. Disciplinary practices refer to the organization of human life in various settings; "discipline" describes the effect that messages from powerful actors, like teachers, have on people who pass through these institutions, like students. The essential reason why I draw on this framework is that it can be productively used to show how teachers' practices with digital technology can affect students regardless of their social origin. Disciplinary practices, in the form of teachers' routine messages to students about their digital play, can uplift students (transform kids' digital skills into cultural capital) as well as systematically hold them back (deny cultural capital).

At Heathcliff Academy, the school serving mostly wealthy and White youth, faculty invoked a view of digital technologies as productive "portals" into the lives of their students. They used iPads, interactive whiteboards, cloud-based software, and even video games to bolster students' creative potential through online collaboration and digital production. In interviews, teachers described students' youth cultural pursuits online as necessary to schooling. Playing online, through either online writing, video game playing, or YouTube creations, was seen as innovative and critical to classroom success. This played out during instruction, too. Teachers frequently deferred to students' expertise with technology, encouraged them to regularly present their online interests in front of the class, and created opportunities to replace traditional assignments with kids' new media productions. Heathcliff teachers disciplined play by transforming it into cultural capital for achievement.

At Sheldon Junior High, the school serving mostly middle-class and Asian American youth, faculty constructed digital technologies as high-stakes platforms for traditional tests, as well as tools for student surveillance and punishment. Administrators opted not to purchase interactive whiteboards because they wanted faculty to constantly roam around the classroom and monitor student behavior. On top of that, teachers and administrators actively lurked on students' accounts to police many of the same playful activities that were validated at Heathcliff. Students were reprimanded for playing online, like perusing YouTube videos, playing video games, or even communicating with their peers using text-messaging software. Online play was seen as deleterious to classroom achievement. Instead, teachers used cloud-based technology to create online quizzes or other activities that pitted students against one another. Sheldon teachers disciplined play by rendering it threatening to learning, and therefore cut off opportunities to transform students' digital skills into cultural capital for achievement.

At César Chávez Middle School, the institution serving mostly working-class and Latinx youth, teachers saw digital technologies as key tools that students would use in what they imaged to be a twenty-first-century factory. They emphasized students' need to develop "basic skills" with these technologies, skills that included many of the celebrated literacies at Heathcliff, like programming basics, use of presentation software, and new media production. But a critical difference is that Chávez faculty saw students' digital play as irrelevant to learning. This meant that teachers communicated to students that their creative expressions online, including social media use, video games, and peer communications, would not help them do well in school or in a future job. By disciplining play in this way, teachers prevented it from becoming cultural capital for achievement. Instead, what counted was students' proficiency in skills needed for rote digital labor.

Disciplining play is how schools reproduce inequality in the twenty-first century. Children come to school with a similar set of baseline digital skills they have developed from play with peers, such as knowing how to communicate online, as well as how to create and share digital media. This presents an opportunity for cultural mobility, one that may potentially circumvent our existing theories that suggest that children's unequal childhoods lead to later stratification in achievement. I found that teachers invoked an orientation to digital technology and students' online play and enacted this perspective with students during instruction. Kids' digital know-how was shut down at schools serving working-class youth and students of color, whereas it was transformed into cultural capital for achievement at a school serving more privileged White youth. These divergent pedagogical approaches to play determined whether kids' digital play was activated into cultural capital or not. But *why* did teachers do this?

WHERE DISCIPLINARY ORIENTATIONS COME FROM

Social reproduction theory points to teachers' perceptions as a key driver of social stratification in education.[13] As the story goes, teachers assume wealthy children are destined for leadership jobs, while relegating working-class kids to the factory floor. As a result of these perceptions, teachers subconsciously guide their students toward these paths during day-to-day classroom life. The end result is that students develop class-differentiated self-concepts, career aspirations, and educational habits that turn wealthy students into upwardly mobile leaders and push working-class students toward working-class jobs. But as I interviewed teachers for this study, I felt as though this argument wasn't fully lining up. The first sign of this was when I asked teachers to describe their student body: faculty would share multiple, conflicting stereotypes about the abilities and potential of their students of color in interviews but acted upon only a single stereotype in the classroom and elsewhere at school.

What I documented from interviewing the predominately White faculty at each school was that nearly all shared two competing views of their students of color—two ways of perceiving working-class Latinx students, and two constructions of middle-class Asian American students. Faculty at Chávez described their students as "benevolent immigrants," but when describing working-class Latinx students elsewhere, they referred to them as "future gang members." Teachers at Sheldon portrayed their Asian students as "cutthroat hackers" but reflected that Asian students they had taught elsewhere were "model minorities." Not only did social reproduction theory not consider how imagery associated with student race-ethnicity would play into teacher perceptions, but it also failed to predict that teachers could exhibit multiple, contradictory perceptions of similar student demographics. This would seem to throw a wrench into theory replicability.

If education scholars had paid more attention to the sociological literature on race and ethnicity, we would have known that teachers exhibit a range of stereotypes of students of color. For example, some studies find that some teachers construct working-class Latinx students as hardworking immigrants, while others view students who are Latinx as having criminal intents. Other studies show teachers constructing upwardly mobile Asian-American students as model minorities, or bound for success as a consequence of racial affiliation, whereas some work portrays such youth as cutthroat competitors.[14] I, too, observed diversity in the types of cultural imagery teachers drew upon to construct their students of color.

What also makes race a particularly important aspect here is that despite exhibiting multiple sets of stereotypes about students of color, teachers at each school did not have any comparable racialized imagery to describe their White students. Teachers would not describe their students as "White students" but rather referred to White students only by their individual names. When asked about White students, teachers' take was that they were unique and could not be generalized about, despite having just generalized about their Asian and Latinx students earlier in the interview.

Fortunately, theories of colorblind racism fill in the gaps left by class-focused editions of social reproduction theory. Theories of colorblind racism argue that contemporary racial ideology arms Whites with tools to "not see color" while simultaneously asserting very problematic racist perceptions and practices that benefit Whites at the expense of people of color.[15] One way that colorblind racism does this is through Whites' racial stereotyping.[16] Racial stereotypes allow teachers to attribute particular assumptions (like academic performance) about their students to inferences about the collective experience of that student's entire racial-ethnic group. These stereotypes then provide a lens for interpreting pedagogical needs in the classroom, encouraging teachers to instruct students not as individuals but rather as unfair and inaccurate representations of academic worth based on their racial-ethnic group.

Although some of the racial stereotypes of students in this study at first seem more "positive" than others, even these positive stereotypes reproduce Whites' colorblind ideology. Portraying Asian students as "model minorities," for example, simplifies the lived experience of an entire racial-ethnic population and fails to treat the student as an individual person. Such practice also puts incredible pressure on students to uphold these stereotypes, rendering academically struggling Asian students invisible.[17] It also drives tension between student racial-ethnic groups, pitting the "model" group against others, when in fact the source of such tension is Whites' broader racist ideology.[18] White students, however, were treated as individuals—to make generalizations about them evoked confusion and even anger from White faculty, who felt such generalizations were unfair and problematic. Ultimately this creates an asymmetry in teacher's perceptions of why good or bad things happen to students: "model minorities" are intelligent because of their racial-ethnic makeup, whereas the intelligence of Whites is based on their own capability and individual effort. Further, if teachers socialize this perspective in the classroom, we can imagine it differently affecting students' sense of academic self-worth along racial-ethnic lines.

Although theories of race and colorblind ideology clarify the form and history of teachers' racial stereotypes for students of color, as well as the differential treatment benefiting White students, they did not help me to make sense of the contradictory stereotypes that teachers possessed about the same racial-ethnic student populations. How could it be that the same teachers could describe their current Latinx students as "benevolent immigrants" and yet describe Latinx students they had taught elsewhere as "criminals"? Both stereotypes exist in our society, but theories of race and racism do not explain how dichotomous stereotypes can coexist and still produce unequal educational outcomes.

I ultimately argue that to understand the sources of teachers' perceptions, we need to look closely not only at teachers' relationships with their students, but also at teachers' relationships with other teachers. Although some notable work documents the impact of trust among faculty on student achievement, scant research exploits how faculty workplaces may shape their perceptions of students of different races and classes.[19] Much of education literature initially gave me a kind of tunnel vision as I studied these schools: all my questioning and observations were focused on students and teachers' interactions with students. But the true beauty of ethnographic work is that I could not ignore the terrific gossip, stories of camaraderie, and tales of workplaces past shared by teachers in the faculty lunchroom and elsewhere at school. The faculty in this study inadvertently guided me toward research on organizational culture.

School-focused work in the literature on organizational culture argues that faculty workplaces host norms shared by teachers. These norms are not necessarily brought by teachers to the school, but rather emerge from the history of the school and are situated in a particular setting. Existing work on this topic examines whether schools differ in whether teachers are collaborative with one another or instead more hostile. Differences along these dimensions indeed exist by school and predict student achievement. At workplaces where faculty collaborate, student race and class gaps in achievement are lessened; at schools where faculty are less collaborative and more hostile to one another, student race and class gaps in achievement are aggravated.[20]

With the data from this study, I can't pinpoint where teachers obtained racialized and classed stereotypes of their students, but I *can* show whether teachers possessed those stereotypes and how they deployed them at school. In this study, I find that in the context of an interview, teachers displayed awareness of multiple constructions of Asian American youth as either model minorities or Tiger Mom-raised, cutthroat hackers. But I find that only teachers at Heathcliff saw their Asian American students as the former and only teachers at Sheldon saw them as the latter. Teachers at Heathcliff shared an orientation of serving elites (their students) as a consequence of parental pressures. This workplace dynamic aligned with the model minority imagery they described during interviews. At Sheldon, however, teachers shared a threat orientation to their students as a consequence of how faculty interpreted neighborhood demographic shifts as a violation of their racial and social boundaries. This view of students as threats aligned with the cutthroat hacker imagery they described during interviews.

Faculty also reported a similar set of beliefs about Latinx students as either benevolent immigrants or future gang members, but only teachers at Chávez saw their Latinx students as the former and only teachers at Sheldon saw them as the latter. Teachers at Chávez shared a caretaker orientation to their students as an extension of the family-like, "in it together" mentality that carried over from their transition from an elementary school to a middle school. This caretaker orientation aligned with the benevolent immigrant imagery teachers described during interviews. At Sheldon, however, the aforementioned threat orientation also applied to their Latinx students, and faculty at that school thus drew upon future gang member stereotypes.

Faculty workplace norms and teachers' perceptions of students of color are directly related and drive their disciplinary approach to kids' digital play. Sheldon faculty reported their workplace as "every man for himself": rife with hostility, teacher-to-teacher surveillance, and competition. The fractious dynamic among Sheldon faculty drove perceptions of middle-class Asian American youth as "cutthroat hackers" and their smaller population of Latinx students as "future gang members." Teachers at Sheldon therefore saw kids' digital play as inherently threatening to schooling, and they disciplined play for the youth of color by denying its potential as cultural capital for achievement. Chávez faculty reported their workplace as "in it together," a family-like dynamic of support and collaboration. The "in it together" dynamic among Chávez faculty drove perceptions of working-class Latinx youth as "hardworking immigrants"; teachers thus saw kids' digital play as nonthreatening but irrelevant. Teachers instead confined school-sanctioned activities to rote digital labor they believed would help their students get jobs someday as contemporary worker bees.[21]

An interesting consequence of colorblind racism is that the invisibility of Whiteness privileged White students, no matter the school context. Literature in this space argues that Whiteness is not typically seen day-to-day as a racial identity or categorization, but is rather collectively seen as "normal" and muted, whereas other minoritized groups are systematically marked. As a consequence, the actions of Whites are seen as individual whereas those of people of color are interpreted as a representation of their racial-ethnic group. This played out exactly in Sheldon and Heathcliff, the two schools with White students, but in a paradoxical way. White students' successes at Heathcliff were seen as a result of their individual achievement, whereas Asian students' successes were seen as a result of being Asian ("model minority"). Asian and Latinx students' bad behavior at Sheldon was seen as a result of being Asian (Tiger Mom-raised hacker) or Latinx ("future gang member"), whereas White students were predominately ignored or punished less severely. The invisibility of Whiteness both elevated White students and shielded them from potential sanctions that students of color experienced.

Education research on teachers' beliefs has largely been conducted in a separate domain from that on school workplace culture. I address the puzzle of where teachers' disciplinary orientations to children's play come from by showing how teachers' beliefs and faculty workplace dynamics interact with one another. Let's talk next about the ways in which these perceptions, and resultant disciplinary approaches to digital play, differently socialized children as digital actors in and outside of school.

SCHOOLS AS SOCIALIZING AGENTS FOR DIGITAL PARTICIPATION

I had always planned for a chapter exclusively using interviews with students to understand how they experience the school structures I document in the rest of the book. Initially, I pursued a thread, guided by sociologists of education and internet researchers, to understand what shapes whether students take advantage of resources available online. Online resources, which could be anything from online news, politics, government resources, or art, have been described by some researchers as "capital-enhancing" activities that could help drive educational outcomes, much like their offline counterparts. Certainly, understanding whether students are differently coached into taking advantage of such resources would reveal a digital inequity worth addressing.

One of the most longstanding lessons I have learned from interviews with kids is that they will straight up tell you when you are missing the real story. They taught me that it isn't a simple matter of being coached to seek out the "right" content or activities online. It's also about the powerful role schools' disciplinary orientations play in shaping not just whether but also *how* students participate online in ways that may lead to unequal gains. I found that students from Heathcliff curated a professional identity online aimed at conveying readiness for elite colleges and universities, whereas students from Chávez created and shared primarily for friends and exhibited little institutionally minded savvy in how they presented themselves online. Sheldon students, however, hid their identities online for fear of teacher reprimand, leaving few digital traces for future colleges or employers aside from their school records.

These reactions matter because they unpack a critical aspect of what scholars term an online "participation gap" by making a sociological connection to school socialization. Media scholars argue that people arrive at information-rich online environments with an unequal distribution of resources, or the know-how to effectively find and take advantage of important online information or online learning experiences. Quantitative work is even starting to see demographic differences in online participation: wealthier people seem more likely than those less well-off to use the internet to learn stock prices, check economic and political news, use email, use search engines, and access health information. Socioeconomic status and gender are associated with different likelihoods of creating and sharing media or information online, rather than simply consuming it. These worrying differences in participation along lines of socioeconomic status, gender, and education are seen by internet scholars as a signal of potential inequities. A contribution of this chapter is to understand not only how schools affect whether students access these online resources but also how students differently learn how to curate online presences that might lead to unequal outcomes.

Fully understanding kids' digital practices requires understanding the contemporary playing field for online participation. Fortunately, internet scholars have also done some of this theoretical work for us by fleshing out a concept called *networked publics*, or the many stages for interaction online that connect people locally and globally.[22] Drawing on Erving Goffman, they argue that people navigate networked publics strategically, because shared media or interactions online bleed into other contexts, including not only other websites, social media networks, and online communities, but offline contexts as well. Think of someone texting an embarrassing photo of you to a group of friends—someone could save that photo, upload it to a social media network, and who knows who could see it after that point? As explained in chapter 4, "networked publics" refers to the many, many online contexts that exist and may at any point connect digital traces to other audiences. What's fascinating is that I find school-level differences in how teachers socialize students into particular strategies for navigating networked publics.

Teachers' disciplinary approach to their students' digital play is a mechanism that drives school-level differences in how these kids learn to participate online. Recall that at César Chávez (predominately working-class Latinx youth) teachers disciplined students' digital play by communicating that it was *irrelevant* to school. In turn, students came to think of play as distinctly separate from, and irrelevant to, school. Youth then pursued fun-filled activities online, like gaming, media making, and music creation, with their friends as the primary audience. Faculty at Heathcliff Academy (predominately wealthy and White youth) instead disciplined digital play by communicating to their students that digital play was *essential* to school. As a result, digital play became inseparable from school, and these youth curated their online identities, including interests in activities like gaming, as well as cosmopolitan affinities like gymnastics, debate, and Krav Maga. They did so while heeding the possibility that teachers and future college admissions officers might see their activities. Teachers at Sheldon (predominately middle-class Asian youth) disciplined digital play by communicating to students that their play was *threatening* to school. Like Chávez youth, Sheldon students also came to think of play as distinctly separate from school, but went to considerable lengths to hide their digital traces online: locking their social media accounts from the public or using apps that allowed them to ghost, or participate online, in ways that left little evidence that they were there. They did so to avoid discovery by their teachers, who would punish them for "messing around," as they regularly observed happened to other students. These students said that their hope was that future colleges would reflect only on their school records, given their tightly regulated approach online.

This suggests that disciplining play is a teacher-driven form of socialization, and the work that this socialization does is to create a symbolic boundary between "school" and "play" that affects how students see the relationship between their own creative work and educational institutions. A by-product of such a relationship is that students develop normative interpretations as to whether digital play is *appropriate* online and, if so, whether the intended audience should include education officials like teachers, college admissions officers, and future employers. Further, these differences occurred along lines of student race-ethnicity and social class, with only Heathcliff's wealthy and White children curating a digital identity not unlike a resume for future colleges.

The students in this study help us to unpack internet scholars' quantitatively observed digital participation gaps by revealing the role that schools serve in shaping whether young people participate online, with variance along lines of student race-ethnicity and social class. But these youth also injected a sociological perspective into this work— namely, *how* they participate is just as critical as whether they go online at all. Specifically, the students in this study variably participated online depending on the audience. Online environments are not simply places where students can obtain information, access government resources, or see art, as the literature on online "capital-enhancing" activities suggests. They are stages where kids' interactions endure online, potentially forever—and the students in this study showed signs of being differently coached for whether they should be participating online in ways that look good for educational institutions or not.

In what follows, I discuss the theoretical and practical consequences of this and findings from the other chapters in this book, working backward from students' online play, to teacher workplace cultures, to the cultural ramifications of disciplining play in education. Although this book is not meant to be a handbook of applied solutions to the discussed issues, I conclude this chapter by attempting to translate, in plain terms, how the themes of this book apply to key stakeholders: teachers, including curriculum designers, teacher professional development administrators, parents and caregivers, and education technologists.

STUDENT CREATIVITY AND ALIENATION

A careful reader will notice that many of the phenomena described in this book could occur without digital technology present, as well. The mechanisms I document—teachers' messages to students about the value of their play, teacher workplaces, and organizational culture—likely occur even when digital technologies are absent. The focus on social dynamics that inform whether student play is activated or not as cultural capital for success is what makes this project sociological. This "digital era" simply provided an important setup to test theories of unequal childhoods and cultural inequality in education. It allowed me to show processes of alienation that affect young people at school that cannot entirely be attributed to inequities in child-rearing practices.

Social reproduction theorists in education rely heavily on Marx's theory of class domination to explicate processes of alienation through schooling. A central component of his theory is that institutions dominate human beings by regulating workers' creativity. Marx argues that workers' true creative selves are warped and suppressed such that waking hours are devoted to rote factory labor in the interest of subpar reward. The bourgeois who ran these factories created the conditions in which the working class systemically experienced a loss of self on the shop-room floor. Bowles and Gintis famously ran with this idea when articulating social reproduction theory in education. As the argument goes, schools serving different student class populations socialize children into different habits, skills, and notions of self-worth. Wealthy children are taught to be determined CEOs who see opportunities, take creative risks, and cash in; middle-class children are taught to be managers who keep the ship running; and working-class children are taught to be factory laborers. School socialization works by depositing in children durable sets of habits and dispositions, such as aspirations, academic self-confidence, and approaches to schoolwork that guide them to different academic trajectories and class-distinct outcomes in the labor market.

Sociologists often treat digital technologies today as quite different from the factory technologies studied by academics past. In my mind, they're essentially the same in that they are artifacts that can be adopted as part of capitalist processes. A central goal of this study was to tease out whether and how digital technologies were variably taken up by schoolteachers and invoked in ways that lead to social reproduction. Sadly, despite teachers' best intentions, I find that they were. As I tried to understand how digital technologies were used in these schools, I learned something about social reproduction that Bowles and Gintis missed but that Marx knew all along: an essential component of school socialization is that the "inner supervisor" implanted by teachers in students' consciousness is a particular configuration of "work" and "play" in institutionally sanctioned contexts. This internalized boundary between work and play is how culture drives action, not only inside schools but outside school and even online, in ways that appear to differ by students' race-ethnicity and class.

The best parallel to these findings is in work by Paul Willis.[23] He found that teachers treated working-class and middle-class high school students differently, and in ways that led the former to differentiate themselves from school culture and the latter instead to integrate with it. This varied differentiation and integration was what caused students to develop different tastes in postgraduate working environments: working-class students favored the factory room shop floor, as it felt familiar and validating of the culture in which they had participated as a result of teachers' class-based marginalization. I see the present study as adding to this work in several ways. First, by conducting a comparative study of three schools, I showed how the story is not just one of within-school stratification. It occurs *between* schools as well: teachers do not need to segregate within their own school to contribute to system-level social stratification. Second, I show that social class is just one aspect of a broader system of statuses, including race-ethnicity, on which teachers draw to regulate children. Third, by studying middle schools, rather than high schools, I can focus on kids' play at a time when it is highly formative in their development. Watching teachers discipline kids' play starting at ten years old and then comparing how ten-year-olds and fourteen-year-olds talk about their creative self-worth to teachers is compelling. It tells me that integration and differentiation is in many ways grounded in how children differently learn to see play (their creative selfhood) as important to schooling.

Further, when thinking about the different configurations of work and play that students at each school in this study developed, I am unconvinced that any student—wealthy or working-class, White, Asian, or Latinx—truly "wins." Certainly the predominately wealthy and White students at Heathcliff were being cultivated for continued upward mobility. But again, I think that Marx was right in that the institutional processes of domination warp anyone touched by the system.[24] Remember that Marx's theory of alienation refers to the estrangement humans experience in a stratified society. Factory workers, like the working-class Latinx students in this study, are forced to see their creative self-worth as unwelcome on the job. This is an example of what Marx would describe as alienation, or an unnatural regulation of creativity that renders factory workers hollow shells who slave for hours to build products with which they have no meaningful connection. As I interviewed students at Heathcliff Academy, I noticed that they had developed an eerie sensibility, one that suggested their creative selfhood mattered only insofar as it conveyed moral worth to powerful officials like those in educational institutions.[25] This was dramatically different from how students at César Chávez Middle School described their play outside of school, like making online music with cousins or creating worlds within *Minecraft* with friends. There was a huge and critically important power differential in that Heathcliff students were more or less being guided toward continued economic security, while Chávez students were guided toward working-class jobs. Still, I would argue that even Heathcliff students experienced some alienation in that their creative selfhood had been merged with the educational institution: they were only as worthwhile as they were in the eyes of the system.

What I hope to convey here is that disciplining play creates incredibly high stakes for children in that it shapes whether they will view their own creative selves as important or not. In other words, disciplining play is a method of alienation that serves as a mechanism for social reproduction in education.

THEORIES OF CULTURAL RESOURCES AND DIGITAL DISTINCTIONS

Another goal of this book was to unpack some of our thinking as sociologists of education studying cultural resources. So much of education research on culture rests on notions of unequal childhoods, or the idea that children arrive at school with class-based differences in habits and skills that result in unequal gains. One problem with this approach is that many misinterpret it to mean that parents need to raise their children differently, that poor families need to learn how to teach their kids the things that wealthy families do.[26] This mistakenly places the burden on families. Poor parents are thought to need to "do better" in giving their kids the resources they need to succeed. In fact, Bourdieu really meant that the problem is the educational institution. Teachers grade children based on standards of achievement shared by wealthier people (not simply how they do on a test, but when and how they ask for help, the types of interests they exhibit, etc.).

The other problem is that we as Bourdieuians have done a terrible job exploring the relationship between race and class, or intersections of other statuses more generally.[27] With few exceptions, the argument we're left with from work on cultural capital in education is that if both a working-class Latinx child and a working-class White child learned the same valued cultural resources, they would both achieve. This is, at its core, the theory of cultural mobility. In this book, I use the case of digital skills to flatly show that this theory of cultural mobility is false. I believe that the original thinking here suffers from a misinterpretation of Bourdieu. The "rules of the game," so to speak, enforced by educational institutions (Bourdieu refers to this as a social field)[28] don't have to be based just on social class. They could be any set of habits, skills, or statuses as long as they are part of institutional authorities' shared expectations. The history of the US educational system is so deeply intertwined with histories around race and ethnicity that not to acknowledge race in cultural theories of schooling is a disservice to research on educational equity—and, quite frankly, it reeks of institutional racism within our own sociological halls.[29] It results in theories of equity that make false promises of cultural mobility to students of color and their families.

I do not say all of this to discount decades of work on cultural capital and class-based stratification in schools. The sheer volume and replicability of such work clearly show that teachers variably treat class-based differences in kids' skills as valuable to school or not, and systematically reward middle- and upper-class White students over working-class White students. In fact, what I additionally hope to articulate is that I expect elements of this phenomenon to be replicated soon as digital technologies are absorbed into the parenting practices of privileged families. We may soon forget what it was like at the time this study was conducted, when young people were the first adopters of many digital technologies and were widely perceived to be more adept at using technologies than many adults. As cohorts of tech-savvy young adults age and become parents themselves, I expect that institutionally acceptable forms of digital usage will become more widespread among both school authorities and middle- and upper-class families.

My takeaway from this project is that cultural resources are not like a currency you can hand to anyone in exchange for rewards.[30] The students in this study varied by race-ethnicity and social class, and each developed a set of digital skills in online communication, collaboration, and digital production from play with friends online. Despite each student's access to this knowledge, only students at the school serving wealthy and predominately White children were given the right to treat their digital knowledge *as currency* to be exchanged for achievement. The school organizational context determines not only what ideal cultural resources are but also *who the buyer can be* to facilitate the exchange. Working- and middle-class Latinx and Asian American youth at Chávez and Sheldon had the same resources but were not permitted to exchange them for a reward.

What, then, determines who can reap the rewards of an institutionally valued cultural resource? I argue that it is a mixture of teachers' shared perceptions of student race and class interlocking with durable norms that permeate the faculty workplace. The few Asian American at Heathcliff were also told their play was essential to learning. The faculty culture of elite servitude enabled such an approach to their digital play. But faculty drew upon stereotypes about Asians as model minorities and Latinx students as hardworking immigrants to explain why their play mattered, too. At Sheldon and Chávez, the respective faculty cultures of hostility and family-like dynamics were inflected in racialized and classed stereotypes of their students in ways that denied kids the ability to exchange digital resources as currency for achievement. Sheldon's "every man for himself" faculty dynamic led to notions of Asian students as "hackers" and Latinx students as "gang members," and so play was threatening. At Chávez, the family-like dynamic positioned White teachers as patriarchs who "knew better" than the working-class Latinx students they cared for; their play was therefore auxiliary to the basic-skills approach imposed by teachers. Both the norms located in faculty workplaces and the stereotypes of students of color that teachers bring to school interlock to construct a disciplinary approach to kids play. In a way, it's not unlike how physicists study the way light moves through different mediums. Teachers' perceptions of students are refracted as they pass into the school environment, and this becomes the lens through which kids' potential resources are seen.

I want to return briefly to the topic of how digital technologies may get taken up by families and children as adept technology users age. Parents who are more familiar with digital practices will likely begin to develop different standards for appropriate uses of digital technology and impart these practices to their children. I have little reason to doubt that the traditional Bourdieuian model will, once again, take root and impose a digitally inflected iron cage. Privileged families will teach their kids digital practices that are more aligned with what schools expect than those taught by less-privileged families.[31]

I believe, however, that this project has caught a glimmer of what digital distinction might look like, so that sociologists do not miss these cultural clues as they continue to study both the emergence and the consequences of cultural stratification as the twenty-first century unfolds. Digital distinction rests on the differences in how youth navigate networked publics. Sociologists are most familiar with the *singular* public, or public sphere, a phrase first coined by Habermas to describe a level of society that operates as a theater where members of modern society engage civically.[32] People interact in the public sphere by mounting the soapbox in the center of town, writing an op-ed for a newspaper, participating in a community hall debate, and so on. "Networked publics" describes how people navigate the many "theaters" that exist online, all of which are connected by networked technologies.[33] No digital publics are fully private, because public online communications leave traces that can be shared between different contexts.

I find that the children in this study exhibit differences in how they curate their digital footprints online. As a result of teachers' messages about their digital play, these students developed different approaches toward navigating digital publics, with respect to how their digital footprints might be used by institutional authorities to evaluate their worth. For example, Heathcliff students tried to actively curate a digital presence that displayed how capable they were, in terms of both their adeptness with edgy interests (Krav Maga, debate, etc.) and their academic potential (winning writing competitions, championships, etc.). Sheldon students feared that institutional authorities would see them at all, and correspondingly locked down their online accounts in the hope that their performance on school exams would be all that college admissions officers would see. Chávez students were told what they did for fun didn't matter to school, so they engaged in all sorts of digital creative pursuits that were available to anyone who stumbled upon them online. This may have had bad consequences for those students if college admissions officers ran across them.

In sum, I urge scholars to explore how kids' habits in online publics may be differently developed depending on their social milieu, and also to examine how institutional authorities may differently value these online practices. What first comes to mind is, of course, college admissions processes, but I imagine different approaches to online participation may matter in other contexts as well, like digital contexts where people debate content in news articles or social issues, online learning environments, etc.

WHITE RACIAL IDEOLOGY AND SCHOOL ORGANIZATIONAL CULTURE

A central takeaway from this book is one that further extends what educational researchers have argued in different ways for a number of years: simply providing new technologies to students and teachers does not have a direct effect on student achievement gaps.[34] Technology does not inherently create good classrooms; rather, technologies can be *adopted* by teachers and students to meet educational goals. This is not to say that we shouldn't ensure that teachers and their students have access to up-to-date technologies. But the more complicated question is what shapes schools' adoption of available technologies, and in this book I show that a primary driver is the relationship between faculty workplace pressures and teachers' racialized and classed perceptions of students. Teachers' perceptions and faculty workplace dynamics are essential components for understanding how and why digital technologies are adopted in different ways.

It's outside of the scope of this study to document the sources of participating teachers' racialized and classed assumptions about children. It very well may be that assorted beliefs about children were so homogenous because the teachers in this sample were mostly White, middle-class, and female. Faculty may be part of a similar cultural milieu where these ideas circulate, one that is likely aligned with existing theoretical conceptions of White racial ideology. Of note are the few teachers of color in this sample, who sometimes exhibited in interviews different notions of students of the same racial-ethnic group and/or contested negative, mainstream stereotypes about students of the same racial-ethnic group as they identified with.

Regardless of source, stereotypes carried by the predominately White and middle-class teachers in this study are part of a mechanism that serves educational inequality. White students were characterized as individuals, while Asian American and Latinx students were characterized as avatars, or representations, of their racial-ethnic and class statuses. Sometimes these assumptions were "positive," like model minorities or hardworking immigrants. Sometimes these assumptions were "negative," like Tiger Mom-raised hackers or future gang members. The sheer existence of these stereotypes nets gains for White students over students of color, no matter the context. White students' successes and failures were seen as individual and not attributed to stereotypes about White youth, whereas Asian American and Latinx students' successes and failures were attributed to stereotypes about their respective groups.[35] These phenomena are firmly in line with existing work on contemporary manifestations of White racial ideology. Although these teachers told me they "don't see color," at the same time they exhibited very problematic racist beliefs and had divergent approaches to disciplining play that benefited White students while discriminating against children of color.

Whether the stereotypes applied are negative or positive, their application exacts real costs for children's educational development. I won't rehearse here the voluminous work illustrating the consequences of negatively stereotyping students according to their racial-ethnic or class statuses.[36] But to impose even "positive" stereotypes upon youth may set real limits on their potential. Achieving White students in this study learned that their successes were due to their own actions, whereas achieving Asian and Latinx students received messages that their successes were due to work ethics promoted by collective cultures surrounding their racial-ethnic and class location. These kids got the impression that their successes were ultimately not their own. Thus there are real impacts on children's identities and sense of self-efficacy that vary by student race-ethnicity and class. Further, some work suggests that the cost for Asian youth, in particular, is the stress of meeting this "positive" model minority stereotype.

These stereotypes also inherently set limits on teachers' perceived labor market outcomes for students of color. At Chávez, teachers saw themselves as not unlike White missionaries helping the underprivileged. As part of the shared stereotype of their students as "hardworking immigrants" from "broken homes," they assumed that the cultural knowledge and styles that students brought to school were worthless to learning and achievement. In their mind, to truly help these kids they had to teach basic skills needed on a factory shop floor. Despite teachers' good intentions, this was a profoundly focused tunnel vision that guided their working-class Latinx youth to working-class jobs before they had even had an opportunity to aspire to other paths.

A considerable weakness of this project is that none of these schools had enough Black students to be able to provide additional comparison.[37] Although teachers carried multiple perceptions of Asian American and Latinx youth, I noticed that they seemed to have only one stereotype of the few Black students at their schools: "troublemakers." As future work tries to tease out teachers' perceptions and their sources, it would be interesting to compare the relative fluidity in perceptions of students of color. It may be that the boundaries around some racial-ethnic groups, like Blacks, are so strong that White faculty have only one unequivocally negative construction available upon which to draw.[38]

The racialized and classed content of teachers' perceptions of non-White students are one part of a two-piece formula that shapes how teachers discipline play. The other is teachers' workplaces. Relatively little academic work focuses on teachers' workplaces and dynamics among teachers, and when such contexts are studied, the focus is often on how certain team-teaching structures shape student outcomes.[39] Without discounting the reason we're all in education—to understand and improve educational processes that affect students—I think this lack of research on faculty workplaces signals a collective lack of interest in the livelihood of teachers. As I learned about teachers' day-to-day experience working in different schools, their tales of struggle as they sought to secure a tenure-track job in a tight market, and the challenges they faced at their workplace, it became vividly apparent that these teachers generally felt like their stories didn't matter. Faculty workplaces are a rich source of data not only for understanding how school organizations work, but also for thinking about how we can help teachers face the challenges of doing their jobs effectively and achieving a tenable quality of life.

Although teachers brought to school sets of stereotypes about students of color, I found that the workplace environments inhabited by teachers informed the specific stereotypes they applied toward their students.[40] Sheldon faculty entered an "every man for himself" hostile workplace environment, where teachers would attack one another publicly and expose other teachers' weaknesses for personal gain. In this environment, stereotypes of Asian children as hackers and Latinx youth as future gang members made "sense," even though teachers referred to these groups of students as model minorities and benevolent immigrants at other schools where they had worked. Chávez faculty saw one another as like a family, and teachers were expected to collaborate and support one another. In this setting, stereotypes they held of Latinx youth as future gang members simply did not make sense. Instead, they drew upon other stereotypes of Latinx youth as hardworking immigrants to define their current students. This interaction between organizational culture and the beliefs inhabitants bring to school is a potentially fruitful locus of analysis in future work. It would be worth exploring whether such phenomena operate among people in power in other organizational contexts, not only in education but also in other settings like businesses, hospitals, or even law enforcement agencies.

I also believe that this observed interaction between teachers' beliefs and school organizational culture does the work of *obscuring* White racial ideology, potentially even from White folks exhibiting such contradictory beliefs. During my fieldwork, I found that teachers had a hard time even remembering the things they would say (racist or otherwise) when trying to teach their lessons. They described themselves as being "on autopilot," often owing to the mixture of stress, time management, and student management as they desperately attempted to get through their lesson plans. Some scholars refer to attentive focus on social dynamics as *deliberative cognition*, and unwitting, subconscious processing as *automatic cognition*.[41] It's possible that some teachers may be less aware of the racist beliefs they hold and express as they are teaching in the classroom because they are expending the bulk of their mental energy on meeting explicit workplace demands. This mix of deliberative and automatic cognition may make it even harder for White teachers to critically reflect on their racist beliefs. At the same time, I also think that this interaction of teachers' beliefs and school organization culture presents an *opportunity* for challenging and addressing tacit acceptance of racist beliefs in the school environment. If schools could find ways to create a safe environment for faculty to discuss and reflect on their role in contributing to racial ideology—shifting it from an automatic process to a deliberate discussion—then perhaps that may help reconfigure the ways they discipline their students' play.

PARTNERS IN PLAY

As I walked between meetings at work, I felt my phone briefly buzz in my back pocket. Taking it out, I saw that I had received a text from a friend of mine who works in education. He had been a science teacher for many years and now served as an administrator supporting science, technology, and engineering K–12 initiatives. In the text, he shared a news article reporting that a large, nearby school district had gone completely cell phone free and asked for my opinion. In the discussion that followed—a periodic back-and-forth throughout the afternoon as we each went about our workday—we covered quite a bit. I learned that his teacher colleagues thought that "no cell phone" policies were very important. They believed that kids are addicted to cell phones and that giving kids free rein to use them to interact with each other would mean they would just mess around on social media, bully each other, and distract themselves from learning.

The irony, of course, was that he and I were having a thoughtful debate while casually texting on our cell phones—all the while juggling other work projects. We don't typically see adults have their phones taken from them at work, and many of us need to use them for our jobs. Why, then, do we treat young people so differently?

Having observed how schools guide teachers to discipline the value of kids' digital activities so differently, and with such dramatic differences based on the race and class of their students, I fear that restrictive tech policies are not solely founded in worries about addiction, screen time, distraction, and even bullying. These arguments are by no means new: technological shifts throughout history, including the introduction of televisions, phones, radio, and even the printing press, were met with fears of distraction and negative impacts on development.[42] What I learned from this study is that the school context, including not only teachers' assumptions about students of color and of different socioeconomic statuses but also the hostility or supportiveness of the faculty workplace, shapes how teachers perceive the value of available technologies—not just cell phones but laptops, smartboards, and even video games and social media.

While I'm a firm believer that social scientists are much better at diagnosing social problems than solving them, I have a few ideas based on this research that I think are worth exploring in the interest of promoting more effective learning and student development.

I think that we, as educators, need to reflect on what *counts* as literacy when building curricula and interacting with students in the classroom. At the time of this study, I observed varied interpretations of federal guidance on digital learning expectations and saw increasing emphasis on digitized standardized testing as the way to best use new technology. This push may distract school administrators and teachers from the importance of leveraging students' interests (which are increasingly digital, such as social media and video games) and baking these themes into classroom activities. Doing so helps children from all walks of life feel like they matter to educational institutions. Teachers can then find connections between those interests and academic topics.

I also see a great need for more research on the intersection between school systems, data collection and use, and education technology companies. As a result of the widespread administrative use of digital applications, schools now have more data on students than they know what to do with. When the schools profiled here intentionally employed such data, it was used more for surveillance and disciplinary action than to evaluate and improve teaching and learning. I worry what education technology companies will do with the data they collect on students at schools that license their digital applications. Will they give student data back to schools? Will they provide educator-informed analyses of student outcomes to help improve educational programming? What should schools' standards for and approaches to using student data be, both for day-to-day instruction and for evaluating academic programs?[43]

Last, education technology companies should do considerably more to design their tools with teachers in mind. Many of the teachers in this study felt incredibly frustrated by how hard it was to find education technologies and apps that aligned with educational standards and gave them the flexibility they needed to adapt their tools to their own curriculum. There are many ways to better include teachers in the technology design process. Product developers could hire teachers as consultants on these products; they could include teachers as subjects in user research to inform the vision, design, and implementation of education technologies; and educational organizations could work locally or nationally to establish design principles to guide app development. If such principles were made for and by teachers, they could guide education technology startups' work and lead to better products downstream.

One of the reasons why researchers like me study children and youth is that young people are usually given more liberty than adults to play, mess around, and say and do things that adults are not permitted to in our society. It makes for interesting data that serves as a springboard to understanding not just adolescent development, but also human behavior in general. Scholars of youth culture and technologists alike both agree, in some sense, that play embodies possibility: games can allow the players to suspend expected rules and try out different ones, temporarily take on different identities or roles, and practice a way of thinking and interacting that they normally could not do elsewhere in life. Play can help us to see the world differently and come up with something innovative. As such, it's important for us to try to unravel the various ways in which we inhibit play as possibility in favor of disciplining it to reproduce social inequality.

ACKNOWLEDGMENTS

In some ways, I feel as though I had no choice but to write a book about education. I grew up quite literally surrounded by teachers and future educators. My mother, Anne Herron, pursued a career as a teacher and academic director and eventually served as a provost of a community college. Her brother, Pat Herron, was a celebrated high school history teacher. My sister, Jenna Rafalow, and her partner, Bryant Braga, both work in schools: she is a school social worker and guidance counselor, and he is a history and math teacher. School was, and is, life.

But I also developed a keen interest in digital technologies of all sorts, particularly in computers and gaming. My father, Peter Rafalow, was a terrific supporter of this interest; he himself was a "video geek" who studied media production and went on to help produce early cable programming in California before opening his own firm. (Incidentally, he is *also* now a teacher at the college level and trains young artists in video editing.) Although it was not a passion per se, my mother loved her Game Boy when I was a kid. Tetris was her favorite. I fondly remember the quiet hum of music coming from her device (a theme song called "A-Type" for Tetris fans) as we would all wind down for the night. I'd sometimes sit next to her and watch with anticipation while she played the final level.

Needless to say, learning and gaming were two activities that I found a great deal of support for when I was growing up. I was very fortunate that my parents tried to further these interests by helping me to find video games at the intersection of entertainment and learning. I believe this early support gave me the appetite, drive, and permission I needed to follow these interests well into my professional career. Thank you, Mom and Dad!

Parts of chapter 2 appeared previously in "Disciplining Play: Digital Youth Culture as Capital at School," *American Journal of Sociology* 123, no. 5 (2018): 1416–52 © 2018 by The University of Chicago. I thank the publishers and editors of this journal for permission to reuse the material.

I owe much of my development as a scholar to the faculty who cultivated my approach to research. I thank Abigail Cheever and Ladelle McWhorter for introducing me to cultural theory and supporting my academic interests as an undergraduate at the University of Richmond. While at Columbia University Teachers College I was fortunate enough to learn from Nancy Lesko, Aaron Pallas, and the late Tony "Hugh" Cline; they started me down a path of trying to figure out puzzles associated with youth culture and social institutions. Francesca Polletta and Cynthia Feliciano, my advisors and dissertation chairs at the University of California-Irvine, trained me in research design and social theory over the better part of a decade. They also supported my hunches to study technology and youth culture in a field that, at the time, largely scratched its head when it came to digital phenomena. I must also additionally thank Mizuko Ito for including me as a researcher with the Connected Learning Research Network with generous financial support during my graduate career. Mimi not only was an incredible mentor throughout this project but also introduced me to many scholars whose work is also focused on youth and digital learning.

This book has benefited from feedback from a number of very talented scholars and educators to whom I owe much gratitude. I thank Mariam Ashtiani, Edelina Burciaga, Yader Lanuza, Amber Tierney, Jessica Kizer, Paul Morgan, Alicia Blum-Ross, Antero Garcia, Amber Levinson, Morgan Ames, Cassidy Puckett, Ann Hironaka, Andrew Penner, Mark Warschauer, Crystle Martin, Amanda Wortman, Phil Kim, Barbara Ammon, and members of the UCI Sociology Race Research Workshop. Chris Thaeler's close reading and feedback brought tremendous clarity and polish to the book. The suggestions I received from anonymous reviewers for the University of Chicago Press were also invaluable and helped me to greatly strengthen the manuscript.

Elizabeth Branch Dyson, my editor, believed in this project from the very beginning and gave me the direction and time I needed to do it right. I also truly thank her for helping to make space in sociology for research on digital aspects of human behavior. The discipline will be better for it.

Although this project was conducted under the auspices of the University of California-Irvine, I must also thank my colleagues at Google for being such supporters of my academic work. Josh Lewandowski and Laura Naylor, researchers at YouTube, helped create paths for me to maintain my academic work alongside my projects at the company. Further, my collaborations with designers at YouTube have been among the most rewarding experiences of my professional career. They have taught me so much: the art and craft involved in the design of systems; the profound impacts (and limits) of research in guiding applied solutions; and the power of cross-functional teams with passion and a shared purpose. I thank Jason Bento, Lilian Chen, Venus Wan, Lyric Liu, Kristen Stewart, Kristofer Chiao, and Xinni Chng.

My partner, Emmanuel Castañeda, has supported my work since the day we met. His feedback on my thinking routinely makes me feel like he was a social scientist in another life. His family, the Castañedas, are a source of life and energy that truly revitalizes me every time I see them. I also thank Eva Marie for being my companion and supporter in ways more than she realizes. Finally, I thank my sister, Jenna Rafalow, who has been a guiding source of encouragement and an ally through all things.

APPENDIX

METHODOLOGY

THE SAMPLE

As any school researcher will tell you, getting access to schools to conduct a study can be incredibly difficult. At the beginning of this project, I e-mailed all public middle-school principals within a thirty-mile radius of a region of southern California, describing the study and asking for a preliminary meeting to talk about their participation. The project was conducted under the auspices of the University of California-Irvine,[1] and I described it as a study of both the challenges and the opportunities of using digital technologies in education. I followed up on my emails with a phone call to each principal's office and secured ten meetings. During these meetings, I asked about their school's available digital technologies and answered any questions they had about the project. Ultimately, four schools were interested, and I selected two that had key differences in student race-ethnicity and social class. I recruited participation from the private school through a colleague who knew teachers at the school.

Ideally, a study design of this nature would include schools for comparison in which key variables, including school type, technology resources, and student race and class, are not confounded. To address some of these concerns, I first made sure that the public schools I selected were useful for comparison to the private school. These three schools not only had access to high-quality digital technologies for teaching but also were each very committed to using them during instruction. Each school had active faculty initiatives to support instructive technology use and to assess and integrate technology into day-to-day lessons for every subject. This minimized the likelihood that school-level digital divides, in terms of not only access but institutional priorities for use, would shape the results. During the period of this study, California was in the middle of a several-year rollout of new computerized state tests for their middle-school students. I benefited from a state-level transitional period during which the public school teachers said they were not pressured to constrict their curriculum because of testing. Every teacher I interviewed at the public schools said that whereas in years past they may have worried that test pressures interfered with the flexibility of their teaching, they did not worry at all about testing at the time of the study. Finally, while it would have been ideal to compare three schools where race and class were not confounded, this is atypical. Schools are overwhelmingly similar in configuration to those included in this study.

Teachers, administrators, and staff at all three schools were primarily White, middle-class, and female, similar to the profile of teachers for these grade levels nationwide.[2] Students, however, differed demographically by school. Heathcliff Academy students were primarily wealthy and White, with a small percentage of Asian American children. The annual cost to attend was over $20,000, and they offered no scholarships. Although I do not have representative data on parent education levels, interviews with administrators and youth suggested that students' parents were typically college educated and occupied senior-level positions at successful companies. Further, such interviews suggested that parents sent their children to this school to take advantage of its technology focus approach. Sheldon Junior High students were typically middle-class and Asian American (typically first-generation Chinese American and Korean American youth), and a smaller percentage of students were Latinx (typically first- or 1.5-generation Mexican American youth). César Chávez Middle School students were largely working-class and Latinx (generally first- or 1.5-generation Mexican American youth). Student interviews suggested that parents at Chávez were generally not college educated, whereas Sheldon parents were. While much existing work focuses on stratification patterns within schools, this sampling method compares teaching across schools with different student populations. Exploring stratification processes that occur between schools is particularly valuable because schools are often racially and socioeconomically segregated because of neighborhood composition.[3] See appendix table 1.1 for school characteristics and appendix table 1.2 for interviewed teacher and student characteristics.

	RACE-ETHNICITY (%)					FAMILY INCOME	CLASS SIZES	DISCIPLINE
	White	Asian	Latinx	Black	Other	Free/Reduced Price Lunch (%)	Number of Students	Number of Suspensions
Heathcliff Academy	74	14	3	1	8	0	20	N/A
Sheldon Junior High	15	60	16	3	6	10	26	35
Cesar Chavez Middle	5	3	80	8	4	87	27	7

APPENDIX TABLE 1.1: School Characteristics (Percentages Noted)

Source: Data obtained for César Chávez Middle and Sheldon Junior High from publicly available School Accountability Report Cards (SARC). Data for Heathcliff Academy obtained directly from administration.

	SAMPLE SIZE	GENDER	RACE-ETHNICITY		
	N (% of Population)	Female (%)	White	Asian	Latinx
HEATHCLIFF ACADEMY					
Teachers	18 (86%)	61.11	16	2	–
Students	12	41.70	10	2	–
SHELDON JUNIOR HIGH					
Teachers	26 (72%)	61.54	20	4	2
Students	14	50.00	–	10	4
CESAR CHAVEZ MIDDLE					
Teachers	23 (77%)	60.09	17	3	3
Students	14	50.00	–	2	12

APPENDIX TABLE 1.2: Interviewed Teacher and Student Sample Characteristics (Percentages Noted)

	HEATHCLIFF ACADEMY	SHELDON JUNIOR HIGH	CÉSAR CHÁVEZ MIDDLE
YEARS TAUGHT			
Mean	10.89	10.54	10.87
SD	5.40	7.58	6.73
TECHNOLOGY TRAINING			
Mean	0.28	0.23	0.22
SD	0.46	0.43	0.42
GRADUATE SCHOOL			
Mean	0.22	0.35	0.31
SD	0.43	0.49	0.47

APPENDIX TABLE 1.3: Teacher Sample Characteristics

Note: Years Taught is a continuous variable, and Technology Training and Graduate School are dichotomous variables. Teachers responded with "yes" or "no" to these questions during interviews.

I used publicly available school report cards to identify school-wide characteristics to provide additional information, including average class size and frequency of disciplinary issues; student race-ethnicity, social class, and English-language proficiency; and teacher graduate school training, technology training, and years of experience. During interviews with teachers, I obtained their race-ethnicity, training, years taught, and self-reports of technology skill, and I used interviews with students to identify their race-ethnicity. Teachers reported a comparable spectrum of technology skill at each of the schools, with most saying they were proficient and a few at each school saying they were experts. This same spectrum of teacher skill, as well as other factors such as teacher training and years of teaching, was reported at each of the schools (appendix table 1.3).

DATA COLLECTION

This comparative study included in-school observations and in-depth interviews with teachers, administrators, staff, and students. The IRB permitted me to observe day-to-day life in participating middle schools, including classroom observation as well as other contexts studied in other school ethnographies such as hallways, faculty lounges, and lunch and recess areas. At the beginning of the school year I interviewed as many teachers, administrators, and staff as possible at each of the schools. These interviews occurred in their offices. All interviewees in the study received a study information sheet before interview and were informed that the study was about understanding the use of digital technologies and the challenges and opportunities associated with digital technology use at school. Interviews lasted roughly forty-five minutes to an hour each. No gifts or monetary compensation was provided to any study participants.

I observed the classrooms of the teachers I interviewed until the end of the academic year. I typically spent a full day at one school (approximately 6 hours), and then a full day at a different school, and did this for, on average, four days of each week. At the start of each week, I put participating teachers' names into a computerized randomizer and observed their classes, in that order, throughout each week. This method allowed me to more effectively capture day-to-day life at the school by ensuring that I not only spent equal time with teachers but also observed during different times of day and with different classes of students. By the end of data collection efforts I had amassed just over six hundred hours of fieldwork evenly split among the schools.

Many school ethnographers become integrated into the school setting first by building rapport with youth. I became integrated first through my relationships with the teachers at the schools. I learned during my work that teachers at each school were quite used to being observed by others, including other teachers and researchers, and this helped to acclimate me to the setting. I also note that, although I cannot test this assumption, my status as a White, geeky male may have helped me to integrate into each of the school settings. We know from other scholarly work that men in female-dominated spaces are given "passes" for their social etiquette missteps as well as other privileges in their setting of work.[4] Teachers would often warm up to me after they had learned that I studied technology. They saw me as a sounding board for their gripes as well as a makeshift assistant when they struggled with a digital tool. When I asked teachers to describe their students, White faculty very willingly shared racialized, classed, and gendered notions of their students in considerable detail. I noticed, too, that they seemed less willing to share such information if a student of color entered the room, and so I made a point of conducting my interviews with teachers in private settings, where possible.

Over time, students would notice that I was a fixture in their classrooms and would inevitably approach me to ask who I was and what I was doing there. I used these moments as early opportunities to learn about the students and connect with them. Teachers and students referred to me by "Mr.," but I referred to myself by my first name with students when I interacted with them. I also avoided making value judgments verbally about student behavior and was fortunate not to observe any physical altercations between students during the year I attended that may have warranted interjection.

As part of my fieldwork, I not only observed classrooms but also attended faculty meetings and workshops, parent-teacher and after-school events, and also observed in faculty lounges and in student lunch areas. I used ethnographic jottings to document interactions I observed and to record pieces of dialogue from informal conversations with teachers and students. After each observation, I expanded these jottings into detailed field notes. I did not solicit or include data obtained by interacting directly with students online (i.e., texting). Although some students did want to communicate with me across digital platforms, I felt it was too risky given some of the sanctions students at one participating school received for communicating online with their peers. However, I did collect data through observations online on websites hosted by each of the schools, including faculty websites and internal communications tools shared with me by teachers or administrators.[5]

During the last few months of the study, I selected one "ideal type" eighth-grade classroom at each school where the observed school-level patterns were strongest, and I randomly selected half of the students to interview. While I was unable to interview most of the students at the school as I did for the teachers and staff, this sampling method allowed me to speak with youth in classes that were best fits for the school-level themes I identified. The IRB permitted interviews with youth according to protocols established by the school. This meant largely interviewing students in a quiet corner of a classroom or just outside of a classroom at a picnic table. Two schools decided to email parents to notify them that this research was occurring at their school. All students agreed to be interviewed.

Although many ethnographic studies of schools focus on one school or even just a few classes over a number of years, I selected multiple schools for comparison over the course of one academic year. While I could not continue my work in these schools after one year, I found that my data collection efforts yielded school-level patterns.

DATA ANALYSIS

All interviews were audio-recorded and transcribed. I used these interviews to document the various messages teachers and students received about appropriate forms of instruction and learning. All teachers were asked to describe the typical student, parent, and teacher at their school, to reflect on their teaching practices with and without digital technologies, and to comment on students' digital competencies. I asked students to describe the typical student and teacher at their school, to comment on their experiences with digital technology, and to narrate their experience as students over the course of middle school. I then coded these open-ended responses and used them to compare respondents' attitudes toward students and orientations to learning across schools. I present some of these comparisons to highlight patterns documented in the larger ethnographic study.

I conducted an ongoing process of data analysis, regularly reviewing field notes and interview transcripts and writing analytic memos.[6] I used the memos to identify emerging themes in the data, discuss connections to existing research, and pose additional questions. After creating a preliminary coding scheme from themes in the memos, I used Dedoose, a mixed-methods coding application, to code sections of field notes, interview transcripts, and documents. Although obscured from my view while coding, each document was linked to a quantitative data point with sample characteristics (i.e., school name, class size, years of teaching, student race-ethnicity). This method allowed me to code freely for themes and afterward sort coded excerpts by these characteristics to clarify comparisons and identify disconfirming evidence.

NOTES

INTRODUCTION

1. Carlo Rotella, "No Child Left Untableted," *New York Times*, 12 September 2013. Retrieved 7 May 2015.
2. On the state of the digital divide in education and among families, see a series of reports by the National Telecommunications and Information Administration (NTIA) at the US Department of Commerce, *Falling through the Net: A Survey of 'Have Nots' in Rural and Urban Americans* (Washington, DC, 1995); *Falling through the Net II: New Data on the Digital Divide* (Washington, DC, 1998); *Falling through the Net III: Defining the Digital Divide* (Washington, DC, 1999); and *Falling through the Net: Toward Digital Inclusion* (Washington, DC, 2000).
3. "Unequal childhoods" is a well-known term among sociologists of education, originally coined by Annette Lareau in *Unequal Childhoods: Class, Race, and Family Life* (Berkeley: University of California Press, 2011). At its core, the argument suggests that families socialize different habits and skills in their children that lead some children to academic success while others are left behind. As middle- and upper-class families are part of the same milieu as the middle-class teachers at schools, they are able to give their kids a leg up over working-class children by providing valued cultural resources. Thus, upon school enrollment, children's unequal childhoods put children on an uneven playing field.
4. NTIA, *Falling through the Net: Toward Digital Inclusion*; Amanda Lenhart, Rich Ling, Scott Campbell, and Kristen Purcell, "Teens and Mobile Phones" (Washington, DC: Pew Research Center, 2010); Lee Rainie, "Asian-Americans and Technology" (Washington, DC: Pew Research Center, 2011); Amanda Lenhart, "A Majority of American Teens Report Access to a Computer, Game Console, Smartphone and a Tablet" (Washington, DC: Pew Research Center, 2015); Amanda Lenhart, "Teens, Social Media and Technology Overview, 2013" (Washington, DC: Pew Research Center, 2015). It's worth noting that part of why digital technologies are so embedded among young

people is that they appear to have been integrated into their youth cultures. On the rise and saturation of digital technology use among youth, see Mizuko Ito, Sonja Baumer, Matteo Bittanti, danah boyd, Rachel Cody, B. Herr, Heather A. Horst, et al., *Hanging Out, Messing Around, Geeking Out: Living and Learning with New Media* (Cambridge: MIT Press, 2009). Among the reasons for widespread adoption may be that digital technologies have become tickets for entry to kids' social worlds; without access to and familiarity with digital technologies, kids may risk feeling different and alienated from peers. For more on this, see Allison J. Pugh, *Longing and Belonging: Parents, Children, and Consumer Culture* (Berkeley: University of California Press, 2009).

5. There is a long tradition in social scientific studies of education showing that young people arrive at school with unequal resources along lines of social class and race. A central project of this book is to variously challenge and build upon this work, noting specific works throughout. But Annette Lareau has written texts that are among the most well-known on the subject, including *Home Advantage: Social Class and Parental Intervention in Elementary Education* (Lanham, MD: Rowman and Littlefield, 2000) and *Unequal Childhoods*.

6. For a review, see Mizuko Ito, Kris Gutiérrez, Sonia Livingstone, Bill Penuel, Jean Rhodes, Katie Salen, Juliet Schor, Julian Sefton-Green, and S. Craig Watkins, *Connected Learning: An Agenda for Research and Design*, (Irvine, CA: Digital Media and Learning Research Hub, 2013); Colin Lankshear and Michele Knobel, *Digital Literacies* (New York: Peter Lang, 2008); and Cassidy Cody Puckett, "Technological Change, Digital Adaptability, and Social Inequality," PhD diss., Northwestern University, 2013.

7. Alex Dobuzinskis, "Los Angeles School Board Looks at Laptops after Troubled iPad Rollout," *Reuters*, 13 November 2013.

8. "Lack of Diversity Could Undercut Silicon Valley," *USA Today*, 26 June 2014.

9. Jessica Guynn, "Changing the World One Hackathon at a Time," *USA Today*, 26 February 2015.

10. I purposefully use the term "digital youth," rather than "digital native," except when respondents specifically use this term in excerpts. The use of "digital native" obscures effects of digital divides for youth living in poverty. And by positioning children as native others and reifying adulthood as a normal category, it also falls into a line of thinking that anthropologists debate.

11. Plato, *The Republic: Book IV* (Internet Classics Archive, http://classics.mit.edu/Plato/republic.5.iv.html).

12. Johan Huizinga, *Homo Ludens: A Study of the Play-Element in Culture* (Boston: Beacon, 1955).

13. Michael Schrage, *Serious Play: How the World's Best Companies Simulate to Innovate* (Boston: Harvard Business School Press, 2000).

14. Ito et al., *Hanging Out*.
15. Mizuko Ito, *Engineering Play: A Cultural History of Children's Software* (Cambridge: MIT Press, 2009).
16. For a discussion of the relationship between Marx and theories of play, see Thomas S. Henricks, *Play Reconsidered: Sociological Perspectives on Human Expression* (Urbana: University of Illinois Press, 2006).
17. Pierre Bourdieu, *Distinction: A Social Critique of the Judgment of Taste* (Cambridge: Harvard University Press, 1984); Bourdieu, *The Field of Cultural Production: Essays on Art and Literature* (New York: Columbia University Press, 1993); Bourdieu and Jean-Claude Passeron, *Reproduction in Education, Society and Culture* (London: Sage, 1977). For the most clear definitions of habitus and social fields, see Loic J. D. Wacquant, "Towards a Reflexive Sociology: A Workshop with Pierre Bourdieu," *Sociological Theory* 7, no. 1 (1989): 26–63.
18. For empirical work on the stratified rewards children reap at school as a consequence of class differences in their childrearing, see Jessica Calarco, "'I Need Help!': Social Class and Children's Help-Seeking in Elementary School," *American Sociological Review* 76, no. 6 (2011): 862–82; Lareau, *Home Advantage*; Lareau, *Unequal Childhoods*; Annette Lareau and Elliot B. Weininger, "Cultural Capital in Educational Research: A Critical Assessment," *Theory and Society* 23, nos. 5/6 (2003): 567–606; and Shirley B. Heath, *Ways with Words: Language, Life, and Work in Communities and Classrooms* (Cambridge: Cambridge University Press, 1983).
19. On the cultural mobility perspective, see Paul DiMaggio, "Cultural Capital and School Success: The Impact of Status Culture Participation on the Grades of U.S. High School Students," *American Sociological Review* 47, no. 2 (1982): 189–201.
20. Kathryn Zickhur, "Generations 2010" (Washington, DC: Pew Research Center, 2010).
21. Samuel Bowles and Herbert Gintis, *Schooling in Capitalist America: Educational Reform and the Contradictions of Economic Life* (Basic Books: 1976). An interdisciplinary literature on school socialization can be found on the topic of the "hidden curriculum" in schools: see Henry Giroux and David Purpel, *The Hidden Curriculum and Moral Education* (Berkeley: McCutchan, 1983).
22. On schools' structuring role in shaping racial meaning and reproducing racial inequality, see Amanda E. Lewis, *Race in the Schoolyard: Negotiating the Color Line in Classrooms and Communities* (Newark: Rutgers University Press, 2003), and Amanda E. Lewis and John B. Diamond, *Despite the Best Intentions: How Racial Inequality Thrives in Good Schools* (Oxford: Oxford University Press, 2015).
23. Patricia M. McDonough, *Choosing Colleges: How Social Class and Schools Structure Opportunity* (Albany: State University of New York

Press, 1997). On similar class-stratified dynamics for college admissions processes, see Mitchell L. Stevens, *Creating a Class: College Admissions and the Education of Elites* (Cambridge: Harvard University Press, 2007); and Mariam Ashtiani and Cynthia Feliciano, "Low-Income Young Adults Continue to Face Barriers to College Entry and Degree Completion," *Pathways to Postsecondary Success: Maximizing Opportunities for Youth in Poverty* 1 (2012): 1–7. Further, elite educational institutions do more than just provide information about colleges and universities. They aid in cultivating class-based worldviews that students carry with them. See Shamus Rahman Khan, *Privilege: The Making of an Adolescent Elite at St. Paul's School* (Princeton: Princeton University Press, 2010).

24. Angela Valenzuela, *Subtractive Schooling: U.S. Mexican Youth and the Politics of Caring* (Albany: State University of New York Press, 1999).

25. On colorblind racism, see Eduardo Bonilla-Silva, *Racism without Racists: Color-Blind Racism and the Persistence of Racial Inequality in America* (Lanham, MD: Rowman & Littlefield, 2017).

26. On the relationship between school organizational culture and teaching practices, see Sharon D. Kruse and Karen Seashore Louis, *Building Strong School Cultures: A Guide to Leading Change* (Thousand Oaks, CA: Corwin Press, 2009); Stephanie Moller, Rosalyn Arlin Mickelson, Elizabeth Stearns, Neena Banerjee, and Martha Cecilia Bottia, "Collective Pedagogical Teacher Culture and Mathematics Achievement: Differences by Race, Ethnicity, and Socioeconomic Status," *Sociology of Education* 86, no. 2 (2013): 174–94; and Edgar H. Schein, *Organizational Culture and Leadership* (San Francisco: Jossey-Bass, 2010).

27. On organizational culture and such phenomena in school settings, see Kruse and Louis, *Building Strong School Cultures*; Moller et al., "Collective Pedagogical Teacher Culture"; Schein, *Organizational Culture and Leadership*. On the powerful influence that organizational thinking has on how students construct the reality of schooling and their well-being, see Lisa M. Nunn, *Defining Student Success: The Role of School and Culture* (Newark: Rutgers University Press, 2014); Kate L. Phillippo and Briellen Griffin, "'If You Don't Score High Enough, Then That's Your Fault': Student Civic Dispositions in the Context of Competitive School Choice Policy," *Journal for Critical Education Policy Studies* 14, no. 2 (2016); and Elizabeth A. Armstrong and Laura T. Hamilton, *Paying for the Party: How College Maintains Inequality* (Cambridge: Harvard University Press, 2015).

28. A recent exception is in work by Victor Erik Ray where he argues that scholars need to recognize the ways organizations are not race-neutral, and in fact are likely environments that shape racial dynamics and reproduce racism. See Victor Erik Ray, "A Theory of Racial-

ized Organizations," *American Sociological Review* 84, no. 1 (2019): 26–53.

29. David Kinney, "From Nerds to Normals: The Recovery of Identity among Adolescents from Middle School to High School," *Sociology of Education* 66, no. 1 (1993): 21–40.

30. Adam Gamoran and Richard D. Mare, "Secondary School Tracking and Educational Inequality: Compensation, Reinforcement, or Neutrality?" *American Journal of Sociology* 94, no. 5 (1989): 1146–83.

31. International Society for Technology in Education (ITSE), "ITSE Standards: Students" (Arlington, VA, 2007).

CHAPTER 1

1. Critiques of technological determinism have existed for some time, though since the advent of the internet we have witnessed a to-be-expected resurgence of this line of thinking. On predigital technological determinism, see Merritt Roe Smith and Leo Marx, *Does Technology Drive History? The Dilemma of Technological Determinism* (Cambridge: MIT Press, 1998); for a contemporary presentation of this perspective in the digital era, see Paul Dourish and Genevieve Bell, "The Infrastructure of Experience and the Experience of Infrastructure: Meaning and Structure in Everyday Encounters with Space," *Environment and Planning B: Planning and Design* 34, no. 3 (2007): 414–30.

2. On early school rollouts of televisions and early computers, see Larry Cuban, *Teachers and Machines: The Classroom Use of Technology since 1920* (New York: Teachers College Press, 1986); and Cuban, *Oversold and Underused: Computers in the Classroom* (Cambridge: Harvard University Press, 2009). A more contemporary examination of how digital interventions revert to conventional schooling can be seen in Christo Sims, *Disruptive Fixation: School Reform and the Pitfalls of Techno-idealism* (Princeton: Princeton University Press, 2017).

3. A canonical example of the ways institutions shape social reality is in Diane Vaughn's study, *The Challenger Launch Decision: Risky Technology, Culture, and Deviance at NASA* (Chicago: University of Chicago Press, 1996). Vaughn shows how "commonsense" understandings of risk were actually socially constructed, such that anyone outside of NASA would see risk where participants inside the organizations would not.

4. On social reproduction theory in education, see Bowles and Gintis, *Schooling in Capitalist America*. An interdisciplinary literature on school socialization can be found on the topic of the "hidden curriculum" in schools: see Giroux and Purpel, *Hidden Curriculum and Moral Education*.

5. Valenzuela, *Subtractive Schooling*.
6. Prudence L. Carter, *Keepin' It Real: School Success beyond Black and White* (Oxford: Oxford University Press, 2005).
7. Patricia M. McDonough, *Choosing Colleges: How Social Class and Schools Structure Opportunity* (Albany: SUNY Press, 1997).

CHAPTER 2

1. Andrew Perrin, "5 Facts about Americans and Video Games" (Washington, DC: Pew Research Center, 2018).
2. "Internet/Broadband Fact Sheet" (Washington, DC: Pew Research Center, 2018). Other research also shows similarly low gaps in certain hardware access by race, class, and gender. See Paula Fomby, Joshua A. Goode, Kim-Phuong Truong-Vu, and Stefanie Mollborn, "Adolescent Technology, Sleep, and Physical Activity Time in Two U.S. Cohorts," *Youth & Society* (2019): 1–25.
3. Ito et al., *Hanging Out*.
4. On conceptions of digital literacies and their use in scholarship, see Manuel Castells, *The Information Age: Economy, Society, and Culture*, vol. 3 (Oxford: Blackwell, 1998), and Mark Warschauer, *Learning in the Cloud* (New York: Teachers College Press, 2011). Although sociologists do not typically make digital technology the focus of their work, digital technologies certainly "show up" in other extended analyses of social processes among youth, young adults, and in educational settings. See Pugh, *Longing and Belonging* and Janice M. McCabe, *Connecting in College: How Friendship Networks Matter for Academic and Social Success* (Chicago: University of Chicago Press, 2016).
5. Although there are a number of different skills scholars identify as digital literacies, online communication and digital production are both cited as essential skills and are both developed through play online with peers. This makes these literacies ideal to study because kids likely exhibit them and educational institutions increasingly cite these skills as important.
6. On skills associated with computer programming and design, see Ito et al., *Connected Learning*, and Kylie A. Peppler and Yasmin B. Kafai, "From SuperGoo to Scratch: Exploring Creative Digital Media Production in Informal Learning," *Learning, Media and Technology* 32, no. 2 (2007): 149–66. On skills associated with editing and producing media like audio, images, and video, see Rebecca W. Black, "English-Language Learners, Fan Communities, and 21st Century Skills," *Journal of Adolescent and Adult Literacy* 52, no. 8 (2009): 688–97; Barbara Guzzetti and Margaret Gamboa, "Online Journaling: The Informal Writings of Two Adolescent Girls," *Research in the*

Teaching of English 40, no. 2 (2005): 168–206; and Glynda A. Hull and Mark Evan Nelson, "Locating the Semiotic Power of Multimodality," *Written Communication* 22, no. 2 (2005): 224–61.

7. It's important to note that inequities in access to digital technologies still matter a great deal. In particular, some work finds that even as students show increasing access to technology, there are issues of technology maintenance that have an impact on later school success. See Amy L. Gonzales, Jessica McCrory Calarco, and Teresa K. Lynch, "Technology Problems and Student Achievement Gaps: A Validation and Extension of the Technology Maintenance Construct," *Communication Research* (2018). Without discounting these continued inequities in access, the current study focuses specifically on skills learned from play online that students pursued in patterned ways.

8. For empirical work on the stratified rewards children reap at school as a consequence of class differences in their childrearing, see Calarco, "'I Need Help!'"; Lareau, *Home Advantage*; Lareau, *Unequal Childhoods*; and Lareau and Weininger, "Cultural Capital in Educational Research."

9. Bourdieu, *Distinction*; Bourdieu, *Field of Cultural Production*; Bourdieu and Passeron, *Reproduction in Education, Society and Culture*. For the most clear definitions of habitus and social fields, see Wacquant, "Towards a Reflexive Sociology."

10. Some scholars have suggested that we need a new term to describe cultural capital in the digital era. For example, Ariane Ollier-Malaterre, Jerry A. Jacobs, and Nancy P. Rothbard, in "Technology, Work, and Family: Digital Cultural Capital and Boundary Management," *Annual Review of Sociology* 45 (2019): 14.1–14.23, refer to earlier versions of my work on teacher activation of kids' digital skills and note that it is better to describe such activations as *digital* cultural capital rather than cultural capital. Specifically, they say this term is needed because the resources that are activated are digitally related: "the awareness, motivation, and skill needed to perform technology management" (14.3). But in Bourdieu's model, cultural capital refers to the activated state of any cultural form. For example, scholars who study how certain practices at work lead to advantages on the job still refer to the activated resource as cultural capital and not *workplace* cultural capital. This is why I describe kids' know-how or practices as digital but teachers' activation of those states as cultural capital: cultural forms that can be activated could be *either* digitally related or not.

11. DiMaggio, "Cultural Capital and School Success."

12. Sonia Livingstone predicted early on that there may be a downstream challenge in the realm of digital literacies insofar as institutions may have to adopt them as part of their educational philosophy. See Livingstone, "Media Literacy and the Challenge of New Information

and Communication Technologies," *Communication Review* 7, no. 1 (2004): 3–14.

13. Michel Foucault, *Discipline and Punish: The Birth of the Prison* (New York: Vintage, 1975); and Paolo Freire, *Pedagogy of the Oppressed* (New York: Penguin, 1996).

14. Bowles and Gintis, *Schooling in Capitalist America*.

15. On the failures of the sociology of culture to treat race-ethnicity as seriously as it treats social class, see John D. Skrentny, "Culture and Race/Ethnicity: Bolder, Deeper, and Broader," *Annals of the American Academy of Political and Social Science* 619, no. 1 (2008): 59–77. See also Prudence Carter's research on nondominant vs. dominant cultural capital that illustrates how race factors into the cultural "work" that students of color must do to navigate educational institutions. Carter, *Keepin' It Real*.

16. Carter, *Keepin' It Real*.

17. Valenzuela, *Subtractive Schooling*.

18. On the relationship between middle- and upper-class families and children's privacy (especially the privacy of young girls), see Mary Madden, Amanda Lenhart, Sandra Cortesi, Urs Gasser, Maeve Duggan, Aaron Smith, and Meredith Beaton, "Teens, Social Media, and Privacy" (Washington, DC: Pew Research Center's Internet & American Life Project, 2013).

19. At the time of the study (most digital technologies and applications change by the time they are eventually reported in academic publications), Kik was an app used by students on their mobile phones to send text messages. Kik allowed text messaging not just with a mobile phone data plan but also across wireless internet access.

20. Instagram was an app used by students on their mobile phones to view images shared by friends they follow.

21. Snapchat was an app used to send temporarily available images, video, and text to peers within their social network online.

22. William E. Loges and Joo-Young Jung, "Exploring the Digital Divide: Internet Connectedness and Age," *Communication Research* 28, no. 4 (2001): 536–62.

23. Google Drive was an application that allowed users to save their files, like word documents, images, video, and presentations, to an online repository. Google offered a suite of tools within this application, including Google Docs, to create collaboratively written word documents (like this student's creative writing project) and save it to the online drive.

24. Jailbreaking refers to a process by which one overrides the software restrictions imposed by Apple's operating system.

25. APK, or Android Application Package, was a format used by Android operating systems (like the Android mobile phones) to edit or create modifications to the phone.

26. Vine was a mobile phone application that allowed its users to create and share brief segments of video with their followers online.
27. iMovie was an app for editing video.
28. Bowles and Gintis, *Schooling in Capitalist America*, 132.
29. Lawrence Bobo, "Racial Attitudes at the Close of the Twentieth Century," in *Power and Ideology in Education*, ed. Jerome Karabel and A. H. Halsey (New York: Oxford University Press, 2001).
30. Although a deep analysis of gender is beyond the scope of this project, I note that there were some signs from faculty at Chávez that perceptions of video gameplay were gendered at this school in particular. Video games, like *Minecraft*, were described as predominately a "boy thing" (though many young women I interviewed also shared this interest); this activity appeared to be seen by teachers as irrelevant when compared with other digital activities. All forms of digital play were seen as irrelevant to schoolwork, but teachers seemed to view young women's digital activities (not video games, but Instagram, Twitter, etc.) as more creative than young men's online practices (video gaming). This may have gendered impacts on how kids' digital play is disciplined and tracked, much like "pink collar" vs. "blue collar" tracking at school. On this topic, see Nancy Lopez, *Hopeful Girls, Troubled Boys: Race and Gender Disparity in Urban Education* (New York: Routledge, 2003); and Julie Bettie, *Women without Class: Girls, Race, and Identity* (Berkeley: University of California Press, 2014).

CHAPTER 3

1. On the role of teacher perceptions of student labor market outcomes in students' later life chances, see Bowles and Gintis, *Schooling in Capitalist America*.
2. In every teacher interview I asked teachers to describe the student body at their current school and then describe, compare, and contrast it with student populations they had worked with at other schools. I did not name any specific characteristics of the student body (e.g., "Describe the [insert racial-ethnic group] population at this school) in my initial questioning, and probed deeper as all teachers in this study subsequently surfaced meanings associated with student status (like race-ethnicity and class).
3. On the varied constructions of Latinx students, see Valenzuela, *Subtractive Schooling*; Carter, *Keepin' It Real*; Lewis, *Race in the Schoolyard*; Edward W. Morris, "'Tuck in That Shirt!': Race, Class, Gender, and Discipline in an Urban School," *Sociological Perspectives* 48, no. 1 (2005): 25–48; Daniel G. Solorzano, "Images and Words That Wound: Critical Race Theory, Racial Stereotyping, and Teacher Education,"

Teacher Education Quarterly 24, no. 3 (1997): 5–19; and Jessica S.
Cobb, "Inequality Frames: How Teachers Inhabit Color-blind
Ideology," *Sociology of Education* 90, no. 4 (2017): 315–32. On the
varied constructions of Asian Americans, see Troy Duster, Da-
vid Minkus, and Colin Samson, *Bar Association of San Francisco
Minority Employment Survey: Final Report* (Berkeley: University
of California, 1998); Grace Kao, "Asian Americans as Model Minori-
ties? A Look at Their Academic Performance," *American Journal of
Education* 103, no. 2 (1995): 121–59; Gamoran and Mare, "Second-
ary School Tracking and Educational Inequality"; Deborah Woo, *The
Glass Ceiling and Asian Americans* (Washington, DC: Glass Ceiling
Commission, US Department of Labor, 1994); and Amy Chua, *Battle
Hymn of the Tiger Mother* (New York: Penguin, 2011).

4. On colorblind racism, see Bonilla-Silva, *Racism without Racists*. On
manifestations of colorblind racism in schools, see Lewis, *Race in the
Schoolyard*.

5. Eduardo Bonilla-Silva argues that cultural racism is one manifestation of colorblind racism that contributes to the reproduction of this
ideology. Cultural racism includes racial stereotypes that are used to
explain the behaviors of entire racial-ethnic groups without evidence.
See *Racism without Racists*, 56–57.

6. On the negative impacts of model minority stereotypes of Asian American students, see Jennifer Lee and Min Zhou, *The Asian American Achievement Paradox* (New York: Russell Sage Foundation,
2015).

7. I want to emphasize that I focus here on a gap in the literature
specific to interaction at the micro- and meso-levels—that is, how do
White faculty who exhibit two sets of racial stereotypes select which
to "choose" during their teaching? The literature has already done
a thorough job of documenting various contradictory beliefs about
different racial-ethnic groups, identifying the source of multiple sets
of available imagery in macro-level historical and political shifts in
the United States. For example, Stacy J. Lee, Nga-Wing Anjela Wong,
and Alvin N. Alvarez trace the roots of "model minority" stereotypes
of Asian Americans to the 1960s, when a sociologist introduced the
term to frame Japanese and Chinese "culture," broadly defined, as
sufficient to overcome racial barriers to achieve educational success.
Yet the authors also show that stereotypes of Asian Americans as
"perpetually foreign" persist, with examples that include the intern-
ment of Japanese Americans in World War II due to unfounded
stereotypes that drove perceptions of national risk. For more on the
sources and prevalence of such stereotypes of Asian Americans, see
Lee, Wong, and Alvarez, "The Model Minority and the Perpetual Foreigner: Stereotypes of Asian-Americans," in *Asian American Psychology: Current Perspectives*, ed. Nita Tewari and Alvin N. Alvarez (New

York: Routledge/Taylor & Francis Group, 2009), 69–84; Bic Ngo and Stacey J. Lee, "Complicating the Image of Model Minority Success: A Review of Southeast Asian American Education," *Review of Educational Research* 77, no. 4 (2007): 415–53; Stacey J. Lee, *Unraveling the 'Model Minority' Stereotype: Listening to Asian American Youth* (New York: Teachers College Press, 2015); and Claire Jean Kim, "The Racial Triangulation of Asian Americans," *Politics & Society* 27, no. 1 (1999): 105–38.

8. On organizational culture and such phenomena in school settings, see Kruse and Louis, *Building Strong School Cultures*; Moller et al., "Collective Pedagogical Teacher Culture"; Schein, *Organizational Culture and Leadership*; Armstrong and Hamilton, *Paying for the Party*; Dorothy C. Holland and Margaret A. Eisenhart, *Educated in Romance: Women, Achievement and College Culture* (Chicago: University of Chicago Press, 1990); and John B. Diamond and Amanda E. Lewis, "Race and Discipline at a Racially Mixed High School: Status, Capital, and the Practice of Organizational Routines," *Urban Education* (2016). Another way of thinking about organizational cultures in schools is through how they are related to institutional schemas, or routines and shared worldviews exhibited by the educational institution. In a way, the organizational cultures I document in this chapter are both shaped by, and likely contribute to, institutional schemas that make digital technology for learning a priority (despite differences in how they are adopted). For more on institutional schemas, see Francesca Polletta, "Culture and Movements," *Annals of the American Academy of Political and Social Science* 619 (2008): 78–96.

9. Anthony Bryk and Barbara Schneider, *Trust in Schools: A Core Resource for Improvement* (New York: Russell Sage Foundation, 2002). Others scholars have studied teacher workplace dynamics, referring to it instead as "teacher collective efficacy." See Roger D. Goddard, Wayne K. Hoy, and Anita Wollfolk Hoy, "Collective Teacher Efficacy: Its Meaning, Measure, and Impact on Student Achievement," *American Education Research Journal* 37, no. 2 (2000): 479–507; and Roger D. Goddard, Wayne K. Hoy, and Anita Wollfolk Hoy, "Collective Efficacy Beliefs: Theoretical Developments, Empirical Evidence, and Future Directions," *Educational Researcher* 33, no. 3 (2004): 3–13. On cultures of teacher collaboration and support, see Moller et al., "Collective Pedagogical Teacher Culture."

10. For a discussion of these findings about student racial-ethnic composition and relational trust, see Bryk and Schneider, *Trust in Schools*, 97–99.

11. On Whiteness's invisibility and its impacts, see Peggy McIntosh, "White Privilege: Unpacking the Invisible Knapsack," *Peace and Freedom* (1989): 10–12; Douglas Hartmann, Joseph Gerteis, and Paul R. Cross, "An Empirical Assessment of Whiteness Theory:

Hidden from How Many?" *Social Problems* 56 (2009): 403–24; George Lipsitz, "The Possessive Investment in Whiteness: Racialized Social Democracy and the 'White' Problem in American Studies," *American Quarterly* 47 (1995): 369–87; and Jennifer L. Pierce, " 'Racing for Innocence': Whiteness, Corporate Culture, and the Backlash against Affirmative Action," *Qualitative Sociology* 26 (2003): 53–70.

12. On the pressures teachers of color face responding to the normative weight of racism/racial structures in their day-to-day work, see Glenda Marisol Flores, *Latina Teachers: Creating Careers and Guarding Culture* (New York: NYU Press, 2017); and Flores, "Racialized Tokens: Latina Teachers Negotiating, Surviving and Thriving in a White Woman's Profession," *Qualitative Sociology* 34, no. 2 (2011): 313–35.

13. All demographic and household income data obtained from publicly available data via the US Census Bureau. Comparisons are drawn from data collected in 2000 and in 2010.

14. I want to note, here, that not all teacher gossip was aimed at publicly shaming other teachers. Some gossip I observed and heard about was really faculty trying to gather information to help them get by at a difficult workplace. For an overview of teacher gossip, motivations, and impacts, see Tim Hallett, Brent Harger, and Donner Eder, "Gossip at Work: Unsanctioned Evaluative Talk in Formal School Meetings," *Journal of Contemporary Ethnography* 38, no. 5 (2009): 584–618.

15. Amanda Lewis and John Diamond similarly find in their work that Black students get caught more frequently for breaking rules than do White students at the same school, citing teachers' racial stereotyping as a cause for divergent disciplinary approaches. See Lewis and Diamond, *Despite the Best Intentions*.

16. On the broader phenomenon of teacher-student racial mismatch and its association with drops in teacher satisfaction, see Linda A. Renzulli, Heather MacPherson Parrott, and Irenee R. Beattie, "Racial Mismatch and School Type: Teacher Satisfaction and Retention in Charter and Traditional Public Schools," *Sociology of Education* 84, no. 1 (2011): 23–48.

17. I find an interesting parallel here in work by Seth Abrutyn and Anna Mueller where they focus on how particular constructions of social networks shape social psychological processes that lead to suicidality. In environments where interactions are high stakes and put a social cost on opening up, they see higher risk for suicidality. Although the subject of this particular mental health outcome never came up, the organizational dynamics at Sheldon were similar in that they created a set of costs to pursuing some of the collaborative and supportive dynamics described at Chávez. See Anna S. Mueller and Seth Abrutyn, "Adolescents under Pressure: A New Durkheimian Framework for

Understanding Adolescent Suicide in a Cohesive Community," *American Sociological Review* 81, no. 5 (2016): 877–99.

18. Although students certainly interpret parents' messages in their own way, White parents are certainly creating the context for their children to adopt a "colorblind" racist ideology. For more on this, see Margaret Ann Hagerman, "White Families and Race: Colourblind and Colour-Consciousness," *Ethnic and Racial Studies* 37, no. 14 (2014): 2598–2614, and Margaret Ann Hagerman, *White Kids: Growing Up with Privilege in a Racially Divided America* (New York: NYU Press, 2018).

CHAPTER 4

1. On class-based cultural participation and consequences for educational stratification, see Bourdieu and Passeron, *Reproduction in Education*; Lareau, *Unequal Childhoods*; and Jessica McRory Calarco, *Negotiating Opportunities: How the Middle Class Secures Advantages in School* (Oxford: Oxford University Press, 2018).

2. For examples of how participation in middle- and upper-class activities and/or milieus is connected to academic and career outcomes, see DiMaggio, "Cultural Capital and School Success," and Lauren A. Rivera, "Hiring as Cultural Matching: The Case of Elite Professional Service Firms," *American Sociological Review* 77, no. 6 (2012): 999–1022.

3. On assorted digital "versions" of existing institutionally valued activities, see Eszter Hargittai, "Digital Na(t)ives? Variation in Internet Skills and Uses among Members of the 'Net Generation," *Sociological Inquiry* 80, no. 1 (2010): 2–113.

4. On the sources of students' digital skills as not only parents but also young people's peers, see Matthew H. Rafalow, "Disciplining Play: Digital Youth Culture as Capital at School," *American Journal of Sociology* 123, no. 5 (2018): 1416–52.

5. On the role of teachers in shaping children's habits (socialization), see Bowles and Gintis, *Schooling in Capitalist America*. An interdisciplinary literature can be found on the topic of the "hidden curriculum" in schools: see Giroux and Purpel, *Hidden Curriculum and Moral Education*.

6. On the potential of capital-enhancing activities online, see Nicole Zillien and Eszter Hargittai, "Digital Distinction: Status-Specific Types of Internet Usage," *Social Science Quarterly* 90, no. 2 (2009): 274–91. Although they are not typically discussed by sociologists of education, I'd also argue that both access to health information online and civic engagement through activisms online are also potentially

capital-enhancing activities. On differences in how people participate online when seeking out health information, see Sheila R. Cotton and Sipi S. Gupta, "Characteristics of Online and Offline Health Information Seekers and Factors That Discriminate between Them," *Social Science & Medicine* 59, no. 9 (2004): 1795–1806. On the importance of online activism to participants with effects both online and offline, see Deana A. Rohlinger and Leslie Bunnage, "Collective Identity in the Digital Age: Thin and Thick Identities in Moveon.org and the Tea Party Movement," *Mobilization* 23, no. 2 (2018): 135–57; Jennifer Earl and Alan Schussman, "The New Site of Activism: On-line Organizations, Movement Entrepreneurs, and the Changing Location of Social Movement Decision-making," in *Consensus Decision Making: Northern Ireland and Indigenous Movements*, ed. Patrick G. Coy (Bingley, UK: Emerald Group, 2002); and Jennifer Earl and Katrina Kimport, *Digitally Enabled Social Change: Activism in the Internet Age* (Cambridge: MIT Press, 2011).

7. On the processes of young people's interest-driven learning online, as well as the potential academic outcomes, see Mizuko Ito et al., *Affinity Online: How Connection and Shared Interest Fuel Learning* (New York: NYU Press, 2018).

8. On digital participation gaps, see Henry Jenkins et al., *Confronting the Challenges of Participatory Culture: Media Education for the 21st Century* (Cambridge: MIT Press, 2009); and Morgan G. Ames and Jenna Burrell, "Connected Learning and the Equity Agenda: A Microsociology of *Minecraft* Play," *Proceedings of the 2017 ACM Conference on Computer Supported Cooperative Work and Social Computing.*

9. On quantitatively observed class-based differences in the pursuit of capital-enhancing activities online, see Zillien and Hargittai, "Digital Distinction."

10. On the use of networked publics in studies of online participation, see danah boyd, *It's Complicated: The Social Lives of Networked Teens* (New Haven: Yale University Press, 2015); danah boyd, "Why Youth (Heart) Social Network Sites: The Role of Networked Publics in Teenage Social Life," *MacArthur Foundation Series on Digital Learning: Youth, Identity, and Digital Media*, vol. 119 (2007); danah boyd and Nicole B. Ellison, "Social Network Sites: Definition, History, and Scholarship," *Journal of Computer-Mediated Communication* 13, no. 1 (2007): 210–30; and Sebastián Valenzuela, Namsu Park, and Kerk F. Kee, "Is There Social Capital in a Social Network Site?: Facebook Use and College Students' Life Satisfaction, Trust, and Participation," *Journal of Computer-Mediated Communication* 14, no. 4 (2009): 875–901; and Jeffrey Lane, "The Digital Street: An Ethnographic Study of Networked Street Life in Harlem," *American Behavioral Scientist* 60, no. 1 (2016): 43–58. For examples of learning processes

necessary to participate across networked publics, see Lindsey 'Luka' Carfagna, "Learning to Share: Pedagogy, Open Learning, and the Sharing Economy," *Sociological Review* 66, no. 2 (2018): 447–65; Ksenia A. Korobkova and Matthew H. Rafalow, "Navigating Digital Publics for Playful Production: A Cross-Case Analysis of Two Interest-Driven Online Communities," *Digital Culture & Education* 8, no. 2 (2016); and Matthew H. Rafalow, "n00bs, Trolls, and Idols: Boundary-Making among Digital Youth," *Sociological Studies of Children and Youth* 19 (2015): 243–66.

11. Sociologists actually find considerable overlap between media and communication scholars' take on networked publics and the social fields and stages articulated by sociologists Pierre Bourdieu and Erving Goffman. Online environments are simply another stage that actors, like students, can learn how to navigate. Not only does the concept of networked publics enable scholars to treat online contexts as important empirical sites but it also takes into consideration how they work structurally as interconnected digital stages. The most substantive sociological analysis to this end can be found in Ollier-Malaterre, Jacobs, and Rothbard, "Technology, Work, and Family." They argue that technology management is an important aspect of social life worthy of study.

12. In an attempt to debunk assumptions that kids are naturally gifted at technology (and that teachers, therefore, have little to offer in support of kids' digital skill development), some scholars of learning and new media have suggested that teachers play a really important role in shaping kids' digital literacies. It's not therefore far afield to expect that teachers could also shape kids' digital participation more generally. See Thomas Philip and Antero Garcia, "The Importance of Still Teaching the iGeneration: New Technologies and the Centrality of Pedagogy," *Harvard Educational Review* 823, no. 2 (2013): 300–319.

13. In this study I did not find that students reported that their parents were the source of their digital know-how. But parents clearly play an important role in kids' development more generally and are part of the "soup" that constitutes how kids use technologies in and outside of school. Given the work showing the powerful role parents play in educational outcomes, I expect that parental involvement in technology use will grow exponentially as parents are more and more digitally connected. Further, researchers already show the impacts of parental involvement on certain domains of children's lives. On this topic, see Sonia Livingstone, Alicia Blum-Ross, and Dongmiao Zhang, "What Do Parents Think, and Do, about Their Children's Online Privacy?" (London: LSE Department of Media and Communication, 2018); Sonia Livingstone, "Taking Risky Opportunities in Youthful Content Creation: Teenagers' Use of Social Networking Sites for Intimacy, Privacy, and Self-Expression," *New Media & Society*

10, no. 3 (2008): 393–411; Alicia Blum-Ross and Sonia Livingstone, "Sharenting, Parent Blogging, and the Boundaries of the Digital Self," *Popular Communication* 15, no. 2 (2017): 110–25; and Sonia Livingstone and Alicia Blum-Ross, "Imagining the Future through the Lens of the Digital: Parents' Narratives of Generational Change," in *A Networked Self: Birth, Life and Death*, ed. Zizi Papacharissi (New York: Routledge, 2018).

14. Khan, *Privilege*.

15. Ito et al., *Hanging Out*.

16. There is a long, sordid history of blaming working-class students and students of color for developing an "oppositional culture" (originally coined by John U. Ogbu, *Minority Status, Oppositional Culture, and Schooling* [Abingdon, UK: Routledge, 2008]) to schooling that led to poor educational outcomes. This line of thinking was quickly shot down and treated as a straw man for cultural arguments that "blame the victim" for institutional processes. See James W. Ainsworth-Darnell and Douglas B. Downey, "Assessing the Oppositional Culture Explanation for Racial/Ethnic Differences in School Performance," *American Sociological Review* 63, no. 4 (1998): 536–53, and Lewis, *Race in the Schoolyard*. In the present study we can observe teachers (not students) distancing students' interests from the learning agenda, making learning less pertinent to students' identities than teachers at wealthier schools like Heathcliff Academy. Chávez is an interesting case because the faculty ethos was family-like (not punitive), and so there was nothing for Chávez students to be "opposite" about—the students generally loved the teachers and wanted to do right by them. But doing right by them meant following a paternalistic teacher ethos that favored the pursuit of basic skills rather than digital finesse.

17. There is some recent work on other gendered dimensions to interest in technology (and STEM-related fields) that appear to be the result of peer dynamics; it may be that perceptions of the social relevance of technology and STEM could be the result of shifting stereotypes about men and women among peer networks at school. See Catherine Riegle-Crumb, Chelsea Moore, and Aida Ramos-Wada, "Who Wants to Have a Career in Science or Math? Exploring Adolescents' Future Aspirations by Gender and Race/Ethnicity," *Science Education* 95, no. 3 (2011): 458–76.

18. Among the areas I hope other scholars take up in future work is a much deeper documentation and explication than I provide here on how school structures variably affect students along an intersection of gender with race and class. For example, the young women I interviewed at Sheldon seemed to respond to school messages about appropriate behavior online differently than the young men, with a higher frequency of simply consuming online content rather than creating and sharing content even while ghosting, or hiding their identi-

ties. I had an eerie exchange with one young woman at Sheldon who, when I asked why she only consumed rather than created and shared content of her own online, said she simply had nothing interesting to say to anyone. It may be that teachers' messages about the value of digital play vary by student gender, or potentially that there are peer dynamics also at play informing young women's digital practices. On the topic of the latter, see Catherine Riegle-Crumb, Chelsea Moore, and Jenny Buontempo, "Shifting STEM stereotypes? Considering the Role of Peer and Teacher Gender," *Journal of Research on Adolescence* 27, no. 3 (2017): 492–505.

19. On interracial tension resulting from "model minority" racial stereotyping, see Lee, Wong, and Alvarez, "Model Minority and the Perpetual Foreigner."

CONCLUSION

1. Ito et al., *Hanging Out.*
2. For the canonical text on class-based cultural stratification in education, see Lareau, *Unequal Childhoods.*
3. On the cultural mobility perspective, see DiMaggio, "Cultural Capital and School Success.".
4. I refer here especially to work in the sociology of education that is, by and large, lacking studies even about digital technology use at school let alone cultural processes by which technologies are constructed in school settings. A notable exception is Kenneth A. Frank, Yong Zhao, William R. Penuel, Nicole Ellefson, and Susan Porter, "Focus, Fiddle, and Friends: Experiences That Transform Knowledge for the Implementation of Innovations," *Sociology of Education* 84, no. 137 (2011): 137–56.
5. A great review of this work on technology as having inherent effects on classroom life is in Cuban, *Teachers and Machines*; and Cuban, *Oversold and Underused.*
6. On technological determinism, see Smith and Marx, *Does Technology Drive History?*
7. Dourish and Bell, "Infrastructure of Experience."
8. On cultural capital in education, see Bourdieu and Passeron, *Reproduction in Education*; Calarco, " 'I Need Help!' "; Lareau, *Home Advantage*; Lareau, *Unequal Childhoods*; and Lareau and Weininger, "Cultural Capital in Educational Research."
9. On many closures in digital access gaps, see NTIA, "Falling through the Net: Toward Digital Inclusion"; Lenhart et al., "Teens and Mobile Phones"; Rainie, "Asian-Americans and Technology"; Lenhart, "Majority of American Teens"; Lenhart, "Teens, Social Media and Technology Overview, 2013."

10. The purpose of this project is in many ways to critically evaluate the "utopic" world of closed digital access gaps advocated by many scholars and education reformers. But I emphasize here that I do not argue that issues of access are not important and worthy of study in and of themselves. On this topic, see Gonzales, Calarco, and Lynch, "Technology Problems and Student Achievement Gaps."

11. I use here a definition of discipline advocated by social reproduction theorists, one that includes not simply acts of reprimand but also a process by which institutions impart a durable sense of normativity. Herbert Bowles and Samuel Gintis refer to this as the way teachers install a "built-in supervisor" in kids' heads as a consequence of their daily lessons. Discipline could, for example, be the way teachers validate particular student behaviors and reprimand others. Schools can set and enforce very different standards for validation and discipline depending on the setting, as I find here. For more, see Bowles and Gintis, *Schooling in Capitalist America.*

12. Foucault, *Discipline and Punish*; and Freire, *Pedagogy of the Oppressed.*

13. Bowles and Gintis, *Schooling in Capitalist America.* An interdisciplinary literature can be found on the topic of the "hidden curriculum" in schools: see Giroux and Purpel, *Hidden Curriculum and Moral Education.*

14. On the varied constructions of Latinx students, see Valenzuela, *Subtractive Schooling*; Carter, *Keepin' It Real*; Lewis, *Race in the Schoolyard*; Morris, "'Tuck in That Shirt!'"; Solorzano, "Images and Words That Wound"; and Cobb, "Inequality Frames." On the varied constructions of Asian Americans, see Duster, Minkus, and Samson, *Bar Association of San Francisco Minority Employment Survey*; Kao, "Asian Americans as Model Minorities?"; Gamoran and Mare, "Secondary School Tracking and Educational Inequality"; Woo, *Glass Ceiling and Asian Americans*; and Chua, *Battle Hymn of the Tiger Mother.*

15. On colorblind racism, see Bonilla-Silva, *Racism without Racists.* On manifestations of colorblind racism in schools, see Lewis, *Race in the Schoolyard.*

16. Eduardo Bonilla-Silva argues that cultural racism is one manifestation of colorblind racism that contributes to the reproduction of this ideology. Cultural racism includes racial stereotypes that are used to explain the behaviors of entire racial-ethnic groups without evidence. See *Racism without Racists*, 56–57.

17. On how model minority status renders academically less successful Asian students invisible, see Stacey J. Lee, "Behind the Model Minority Stereotype: Voices of High- and Low-Achieving Asian American Students," *Anthropology & Education* 25, no. 4 (1994): 413–29.

18. On interracial tension resulting from "model minority" racial stereotyping, see Lee, Wong, and Alvarez, "Model Minority and the Perpetual Foreigner."

19. On teacher trust and its effects on student achievement, see Bryk and Schneider, *Trust in Schools*. Other scholars have studied teacher workplace dynamics, referring to it instead as "teacher collective efficacy." See Goddard, Hoy, and Hoy, "Collective Teacher Efficacy"; and Goddard, Hoy, and Hoy, "Collective Efficacy Beliefs." On cultures of teacher collaboration and support, see Moller et al., "Collective Pedagogical Teacher Culture."

20. Moller et al., "Collective Pedagogical Teacher Culture."

21. There are some really interesting social psychological dynamics at play that several scholars have explored albeit outside of an organizational context. For example, some work shows that contextual cues surrounding human imagery with varied skin color trigger different stereotypes that can quite literally be connected to different assessments of a person's race-ethnicity. See Jonathan B. Freeman, Andrew M. Penner, Aliya Saperstein, Matthias Scheutz, and Nalini Ambady, "Looking the Part: Social Status Cues Shape Race Perception," *PloS one* 6, no. 9 (2011): e25107.

22. On the use of networked publics in studies of online participation, see boyd, *It's Complicated*; boyd, "Why Youth (Heart) Social Network Sites"; boyd and Ellison, "Social Network Sites"; and Valenzuela, Park, and Kee, "Is There Social Capital in a Social Network Site?"

23. Paul Willis, *Learning to Labor: How Working Class Kids Get Working Class Jobs* (London: Saxon House, 1977).

24. For a discussion of the relationship between Marx and theories of play, see Henricks, *Play Reconsidered*. See also, of course, his original texts: Karl Marx, *The Marx-Engels Reader*, ed. Robert C. Tucker (New York: W. W. Norton, 1978).

25. As I note in the fourth chapter, Shamus Khan describes a similar phenomenon among students at an elite private school I would also call "eerie," in that students exhibited a "performance of ease," or a set of embodied dispositions and affect, that to the analyst feels like an institution contortion of childhood and student identity. See Khan, *Privilege*.

26. For just one example of how Bourdieu's works have been misinterpreted to put the burden on poor families of color for student achievement, see David Brooks, "Both Sides of Inequality," *New York Times*, 9 March 2006, https://www.nytimes.com/2006/03/09/opinion/both-sides-of-inequality.html.

27. For a review of the historical trajectory of studies of culture and research on race-ethnicity, see Skrentny, "Culture and Race/Ethnicity."

28. On social fields, see Bourdieu, *Distinction*; Bourdieu, *Field of Cultural Production*; and Wacquant, "Towards a Reflexive Sociology."

29. On institutional racism in academic and sociological writing, see John Diamond, "Race and Supremacy in the Sociology of Education: Shifting the Intellectual Gaze," in *Education in a New Society: Renewing the Sociology of Education*, ed. Jal Mehta and Scott

Davies (Chicago: University of Chicago Press, 2018); and Paula
Chakravartty, Rachel Kuo, Victoria Grubbs, and Charlton McIlwain,
"#CommunicationSoWhite," *Journal of Communication* 68, no. 2
(2018): 254–66.

30. For an interesting summary of, and response to, characterizations of
Bourdieu's thinking as reductionist or broadly economically determinist, see Garry Potter, "For Bourdieu, Against Alexander: Reality
and Reduction," *Journal for the Theory of Social Behaviour* 30, no. 2
(2000): 229–46.

31. An important difference worth exploring is the rise of "anti-tech"
parents and schools, particularly in areas like Silicon Valley where
such perspectives are starting to emerge. These perspectives are likely
connected to elite cultural distinction in some way.

32. For a review of Habermas's work and his role in contemporary
thinking about publics online, see Craig Calhoun, *Habermas and the
Public Sphere* (Cambridge: MIT Press, 1992).

33. For some examples of scholars' use of networked publics in studies
of online participation, see boyd, *It's Complicated*; boyd and Ellison,
"Social Network Sites"; and Valenzuela, Park, and Kee, "Is There
Social Capital in a Social Network Site?"

34. For a great discussion of this argument, see Mark Warschauer,
"Reconceptualizing the Digital Divide," *First Monday* 7, no. 7 (2002).

35. For more on racial stereotypes and their effect on student well-being,
see Lee and Zhou, *Asian American Achievement Paradox*.

36. For the interested reader, I would start with work on stereotype
threat. See Claude M. Steele and Joshua Aronson, "Stereotype Threat
and the Intellectual Test Performance of African Americans," *Journal
of Personality and Social Psychology* 69, no. 5 (1995): 797.

37. While we are on the topic, the additional limitations of this project
discussed in chapter 1 bear repeating. In this book I periodically
allude to, but do not well develop, how social statuses beyond race-
ethnicity and class factor into disciplining play in school settings.
Rather than make subpar contributions to realms outside of research
on race-ethnicity and class, I humbly turn to other colleagues' work.
Some great starting points include education technology practices
along intersections of gender (Riegle-Crumb, Moore, and Buontempo, "Shifting STEM Stereotypes?") and disability (as an example,
see Meryl Alper, *Giving Voice: Mobile Communication, Disability,
and Inequality* [Cambridge: MIT Press, 2017]).

38. On the rigidness of social boundaries between Blacks and other racial-
ethnic groups, see Michèle Lamont, *The Cultural Territories of Race:
Black and White Boundaries* (Chicago: University of Chicago Press,
1999).

39. On how teacher dynamics shape student outcomes, see Goddard, Hoy,
and Hoy, "Collective Teacher Efficacy"; and Goddard, Hoy, and Hoy,

"Collective Efficacy Beliefs." On cultures of teacher collaboration and support, see Moller et al., "Collective Pedagogical Teacher Culture."

40. On organizational culture and such phenomena in school settings, see Kruse and Louis, *Building Strong School Cultures*; Schein, *Organizational Culture and Leadership*; Armstrong and Hamilton, *Paying for the Party*; Holland and Eisenhart, *Educated in Romance*; and Diamond and Lewis, "Race and Discipline at a Racially Mixed High School.

41. On automatic and deliberative cognitive processes as they relates to culture, see Paul DiMaggio, "Culture and Cognition," *Annual Review of Sociology* 23 (1997): 263–87.

42. It's not difficult to find examples throughout history of figures exaggerating impacts of new technologies on human behavior. See Mitchell Stephens, *The Rise of the Image, the Fall of the Word* (Oxford: Oxford University Press, 1998), for warnings about the damaging effects of landline phones; John Campbell, *The Spectator: A Weekly Review of Politics, Literature, Theology and Art*, vol. 63, (1889), on distracting impacts of the telegraph on daily life; "Senator Marconi's Doubts on Wireless," *Glasgow Herald*, 13 May, 1940, on the "menace" of radio; and David M. Levy, "Information Overload," in *The Handbook of Information and Computer Ethics*, ed. Kenneth Einar Himma and Herman T. Tavani (Hoboken: John Wiley & Sons, 2008), on fears that the advent of the printing press would lead to too much available information, leading to mass confusion and harm.

43. One way to go about tackling this might be to focus on developing really thoughtful school technology plans. Plans are not required at schools, but should be, particularly given the investment required to acquire educational technologies. For more on this, see Cassidy Puckett, "CS4Some? Differences in Technology Learning Readiness," *Harvard Education Review* (forthcoming). It's likely that some teachers and schools may face barriers to developing policies that are student-centered and minimally punitive. Ethan Chang's work provides some great examples of how schools differently approach developing school technology plans, citing one case where the school made efforts to include the community in its decision-making process. See Chang, "Digital Meritocracy: Intermediary Organizations and the Construction of Policy Knowledge," *Educational Policy* (2018): 1–25, and "Bridging an Engagement Gap: Toward Equitable, Community-Based Technology Leadership Practice," *International Journal of Leadership in Education* (2018): 1–19.

APPENDIX

1. This study was conducted under the auspices of the University of California, Irvine, and does not reflect the views or opinions of Google.

2. Emily C. Feisritzer, *Profile of Teachers in the U.S., 2011* (Washington, DC: National Center for Educational Information, 2011).

3. Gary Orfield and Nora Gordon, *Schools More Separate: Consequences of a Decade of Resegregation* (Cambridge: Civil Rights Project, Harvard University, 2001).

4. Christine C. Williams, *Doing 'Women's Work': Men in Non-traditional Occupations* (Newbury Park, CA: Sage, 1993).

5. Although I attribute my social scientific training to many faculty I have worked with, I modeled and adapted my own ethnographic approach under the mentorship of two terrific ethnographers and mentors, Mizuko (Mimi) Ito and David S. Snow. From Mimi's work, I assembled my approaches to working with youth and collecting data from assorted digital traces of interaction online (for more on the approach, see Ito et al., *Hanging Out.* From David's work, I developed a sociological research approach centered on triangulation and local replicability (see David A. Snow and Leon Anderson, *Down on Their Luck: A Study of Homeless Street People* [Berkeley: University of California Press, 1993]).

6. Robert M. Emerson, Rachel L. Fretz, and Linda L. Shaw, *Writing Ethnographic Fieldnotes* (Chicago: University of Chicago Press, 1995).

INDEX

Page numbers in *italics* refer to figures or tables.

and, *70*; disciplining, 3, 8–9, 12–13, 14, 44, 50, 64, 113, 124, 135, 145, 148, 198n37; as irrelevant, 64, 65, 113, 127–28; learning integrated with, 58–60, 114–15, 116, 133; Marxist perspectives of, 11, 25; potential of, 21; as reward, 66–67, 68; social reproduction and, 14, 79–80, 152; as source of innovation, 9–10

policies: "blacklist" and "whitelist," 42; restrictive tech, 120–21, 125, 161

portal approach, to digital technologies, 31, 33, 34, 42–43, 56, 139

potential, of play, 21

PowerPoint (slideshow presentation app), 58–59

practices: digital tools, 23; pedagogical, 3, 14, 15, 20–21

pressures, of parents, 98–99, 100

privacy, 52

privilege: families, 12, 48, 154; White students, 20, 145; of youth, 8, 12, 13, 14, 47, 59–60, 69, 123, 135, 141

processes: disciplinary, 49; interview, 18, 174–75, 176–77, 187n2, 195n4; socialization, 50

programming software, 54

prototypes, 10

publics, networked, 113, 117, 118, 130, 132, 193n11; definition of, 112; Goffman on, 147–48; public sphere and, 155–56

public sphere, networked publics and, 155–56

race-ethnicity, 22, 49–50, 182n28, 186n15, 198n37; constructions of Asian American students, 78, 85, 106; constructions of Latinx students, 85, 87, 88–89; constructions of White students, 84, 108, 142, 143; divides of, 6–7; expectations of, 8–9, 13–14, 97; gender intersected with, 194n18; Heathcliff, Chávez, and Sheldon

distribution of, 27, 170; Heathcliff operation of, 103, 104; privileged parents' perceptions of, 104–5; social class intersected with, 26, 153; theories of racism and, 15, 74, 142; theories of White invisibility, 15, 16, 74, 79, 84, 85

racial ideology, White, 156, 157–58, 160

racial stereotypes, 15, 61, 82, 104, 157, 188n7; "benevolent immigrants," 73, 74, 75, 141, 143; conflicting, 84, 141, 142, 143, 144–45; consequences of, 158; "model minorities," 73, 74, 103, 141, 143; multiple, 73, 74, 75, 76, 78, 83; peer harassment and, 126; "Tiger Moms," 16, 60, 73, 80, 94, 106; workplace dynamics and, 78–80

racism, colorblind, 75, 191n18; Bonilla-Silva on, 188n5, 196n16; consequences of, 145–46; organizational cultures and, 78–79; theories of, 15, 74, 142

Ray, Victor Erik, 182n28

reforms, educational: digital divides and, 4–5; digital literacies and, 28, 134

relational trust, 77

research, 25; ethnographic, 4, 22, 26; methodology of, 17–19, 169–70, 174–77, 200n5; on organizational cultures, 144, 159–60

resources: cultural, 109, 138, 154; inequality of, 112, 134, 152–53, 180n5; online, 111, 146–47

restriction, of peer-to-peer communications, 62

restrictive tech policies, 120–21, 125, 161

reward, play as, 66–67, 68

risks: commonsense understandings of, 183n3; digital forms as, 60, 63

Schneider, Barbara, 77

school faculty: as cliquish, 90; expectations of, 16